CW01432907

PUBLISHING
victorpublishing.co.uk

From Burnage to Barcelona

The story of Cheadle Town FC:
One man, one team and a
world tour lasting 30 years

By Chris Davies

PUBLISHING
victorpublishing.co.uk

from Burnage to Barcelona

By Chris Davies

First published in Great Britain in 2018. This edition published 2020.
Copyright © Chris Davies 2020
Published by Victor Publishing - victorpublishing.co.uk
This version: 2023

Chris Davies has asserted his right under the Copyright, Designs and Patents Act 1988 to be identified as the author of this work.

ISBN: 9798869568564

Victor
PUBLISHING
victorpublishing.co.uk

Acknowledgements

A very special thanks to the following people who have assisted me in the preparation of this book. My good friends Ralph Lomas and Jean Harper. Also to Brian Simpson, David Charlton and Vinny Crolla for photographic evidence. Additional material provided by Doug Welsh, Gary Conner and Dave Stevens.

Cover photos: Grasmere Rovers first home ground was Cringle Fields, Levenshulme, in the early sixties, this shows the dreadful conditions that the early Manchester and District Sunday junior teams very often had to play in. Dressing rooms were unlit, unheated and had no washing facilities. No comparison with our 1980 tour game at the Aztec Stadium, Mexico.

DI STEFANO IS HOST TO MANCHESTER LADS IN SPAIN TOUR

By GEOFF ELLIS

SIXTEEN young Manchester amateur footballers in the world — Alfredo di Estefano, Manchester Junior Football League club who "date" this month with one of the greatest footballers in the world.

They have in their best matches during the London this day in the Valencia area.

One of them will be when he their annual presentation as his manager.

The party of 15 includes three and friends of players and each pays their own costs of £45. Another £40 or so has been spent on providing presents for all the application players in their games, trophies for the clubs and special moments for Di Stefano.

For the purpose of easy telling the Rovers will be known as "Manchester Juniors".

The game against the Di Stefano boys will probably follow the town's fiesta, so a big crowd is expected.

Estle has about 12,000 population and is a town of usual appearance, looking distinctly "oriental." It is well known for dates among other food grown in the hot sunshine of the plains and valleys.

Modest start

The Grasmere tours started in 1941 with a day trip to Blackpool. Next year it was London for a week. Then they spread their wings and went to Belgium and Holland.

Spain was next where Barcelona entertained them, followed by Italy and then Portugal and Spain.

The Manchester Juniors have yet to win a match in these tours, but that is understandable since their opponents have a habit of turning out some of the best young players in their countries.

Many are with the big clubs and have the benefit of professional coaching ... like Di Stefano's boys.

But it is all great experience ... such as happened to one Grasmere lad who was a "new player" and had a wonderful ...

ALFREDO DI STEFANO
season last year following pre-season tour.

Grasmere kick off with draw

GRASMERE ROVERS, playing as Manchester A.F.C., drew D Blanes in the first match of their tour of Spain.

Two thousand people watched the game, which was played under floodlights, and Manchester were applauded off the field after a great performance.

Manchester twice came from behind, Ken Tidman scoring both goals, and 'keeper Eric Bates making some spectacular saves.

Another tour to remember!

AT A TIME when football administrators are looking at any suggestion which might cut down travelling and therefore reduce some of the overheads which are threatening to cripple the less successful side, Grasmere Rovers have just returned from a tour of behind the Iron Curtain—minus a set of green shorts but with a wealth of experience and happy memories.

Their eighth European tour under the name of Manchester A.F.C. was their toughest yet.

The second game in Bulgaria will never be forgotten by the whole Manchester party of 40 people. A pre-match lunch in a de luxe hotel which stood on a cliff overlooking the beach at Golden Sands was followed by relaxation in the spacious grounds.

The game against Bulgarian Second Division side Spartac Varna was watched by a crowd of more than 6,000 people who enjoyed a game which Manchester lost 8—0.

Two goals down in the opening five minutes, Manchester still played attractive football and several times broke through the Spartac defence.

However, Spartac, who spent 15 years in the First Division before being relegated two years ago and failed by one point to return last season were a class above the Manchester side.

After the game both sides exchanged jerseys and a return to the hotel in Golden Sands completed a wonderful day.

Grasmere Rovers have now played 19 games on foreign soil and although they have lost more than they have won, they have gained new friends across Europe.

Grasmere in form

AFTER their recent tour behind the Iron Curtain, Grasmere Rovers have been slow to start the season, but played two successful games at the weekend, competing in the Manchester League, on Saturday, plus their usual Sunday League game.

They beat New Mills Reserves 3—0 on Saturday, feeling that they fully deserved victory after three second-half goals from Ernie Kerridge (2) and Ian Halfpenny.

Against the Saints, on Sunday, Grasmere were two goals down 18 minutes from time, but Mike Ouerden and Ralph Lomas put them level before Ernie Kerridge completed a 3-2 win in the second minute of injury time.

Grasmere get Rumanian runaround

GLOBE-TROTTING Grasmere Rovers, the Manchester League club, were given a Rumanian runaround when this year's European tour took them behind the Iron Curtain.

The tour was arranged through the Rumanian National Tourist Office, and Grasmere were promised they would have two games in Rumania in addition to the two Grasmere secretary Chris Davies had fixed himself.

But when Grasmere, going under the name of Manchester FC, arrived in Rumania no one knew anything about match arrangements. There were no players in the Grasmere party, and they could have done with four games, but as it was they had to make do with two. Both were tough and ended in defeat, but Grasmere welcomed the experience.

The next game was against Rumanian second division side Portul, by Constanta and Grasmere did well to restrict them to a 3-0 score.

The heat, professional opposition and perhaps little too much sunbathing, were too much for the Manchester side.

The second game in Bulgaria will never be forgotten by the whole Manchester party of 40.

Says Chris Davies, "Sir Alf Ramsey and the England team would not have received better treatment. A pre-match lunch in a de luxe hotel on a cliff overlooking the beach at Golden Sands was followed by relaxation in the spacious grounds."

The game against Bulgarian second division side Spartac Varna, was watched by a crowd of more than 6,000 who saw Manchester beaten 8-0.

Grasmere Rovers have now played 19 games abroad.

Foreword

The inspiration to write this book started life ina safari park in East Africa. Friend and author Fred Eyre was lying in a bed covered by a mosquito net when he said to me:

"Why don't you write a book on your travel experiences?"

I thought about it for some time before I decided to put pen to paper. Well, here we are. Thanks Fred for all your advice and help over many years.

Contents

Before a Grasmere dinner with guest speaker Sir Bobby Charlton in 1978

Introduction

This is the story of Chris Davies, an ordinary football-loving man who started a local amateur team and had ambitions to take the team all over the world.

Starting on a muddy park pitch in Manchester, the team went on to play in famous stadiums in Barcelona, Mexico City and New York, amassing 96 matches in 30 different countries, against 7 National teams and before over 312,000 spectators.

The team - called Grasmere Rovers - and now known as Cheadle Town playing in the North West Counties League - toured under the name Manchester AFC and are still the only English soccer team, amateur or professional, to have played in Cuba.

The author organised all the tours as Chairman of the club, and quickly learned that international football tours can involve much more than just playing the beautiful game!

Being caught up in a coup in Kenya was just one of a catalogue of problems and amusing incidents in exotic locations from Povoa de Varzim to Port au Prince and Nice to Nassau.

The story also explains how Chris' fears of flying were conquered and turned into over 400 hours in the air in everything from a small Piper Cherokee to a Jumbo jet.

Many famous names have been involved with the touring scene including Sir Bobby Charlton, Alfredo di Stefano, Pele, Jairzinho, Rajiv Gandhi and Ronnie Biggs.

The excitement of The Stock Exchange is also explained in this story as Chris Davies was a Stockbroker who has spent his lifetime amongst stocks and shares.

It is a story of ambition and a realisation that dreams can come true with dedication and hard work.

Our first ever team photo at Cringle Fields, Manchester 1961

1

Dreams

I stood on the centre circle and as I gazed towards the heavens above and saw the huge towering stands of the giant Aztec Stadium in Mexico City my mind went back nineteen years to Cringle Fields in the Burnage area of Manchester.

We had come a long way since those early days of Grasmere Rovers when we played on a local park pitch with mud and water oozing down the centre of the field, dark cold changing rooms and not even a tap to wash away the clinging mud.

I blinked again and those towering stands became a reality as I walked on the turf where all the top names of world soccer had proudly displayed their skills. This was the Mecca of football where the 1970 World Cup Final between Brazil and Italy had been fought in front of 110,000 seated, screaming flag waving supporters. One of the greatest players the world has ever known, Pele, had weaved his magical spells on the turf I was now standing.

I took a deep breath, which was more difficult than usual in Mexico City where 7,000 feet above sea level altitude is a problem every team visiting this famous city has to endure. How were Grasmere Rovers going to perform on this world stage against a mixed team of ex Mexican Internationals and young reserve players of Cruz Azul, the top soccer Club in Mexico?

It was difficult to realise that this was the 56th game I had organised for Grasmere on foreign soil. That total is now up to

96 and we have played soccer in 30 different countries all over the world, against 7 National teams and have been watched by a total of over 312,000 people.

As we played our first game on Cringle Fields on the 3rd September, 1961, against Sutton Boys, my wildest soccer dreams would never had taken me any further than the outskirts of Manchester. Some of the greatest names in football have been part of the Grasmere touring scene plus some of the greatest stadiums in the world have been host to our ambitious tours.

Way back in 1960 I had been abroad once, to Majorca. I had travelled by train and boat as the Munich air crash in 1958 had settled any doubts I had that I definitely hated flying. The fact that I have now flown 91 times is a remarkable story in itself, but in those early days I had decided that I would travel the world by land and sea.

It had always been an ambition to go abroad and when in 1958 I went to Jersey with my Uncle Alec - by sea of course - I heard that from one part of the island you could see the Northern coast of France on a clear day. With tremendous excitement we went to Goray Castle but I was denied my fulfilment of a dream by heavy clouds and a mist hiding an outside world that seemed to be a million miles away.

Two years later I had my first opportunity of realising that dream. I was a Stockbroker's Clerk and worked for the large Manchester firm of D Q Henriques and Co. That year was a busy one. The Labour Government had promised if they gained control at the forthcoming General Election that they would nationalise the Iron and Steel Industry. Dealings in Stocks and Shares reached a record boom level as the Tories became favourites to win the Election. We worked long days and nights and the reward came with a very generous bonus.

The first time I had ever had a lot of money, so what a time to travel abroad. Nowadays going to Majorca is fairly common. In those days it was really something, but no way would I go in an aeroplane. It now takes two hours to fly into Pahna airport from England. Going by train and boat took almost three days! I went with a friend of mine Raymond Hancock and as we sailed from

Folkestone the dream I had had for years became reality. The coast of Northern France came nearer and nearer. This was the new world I had wanted to see. My first step on foreign soil in Boulogne was one I will always remember.

We went by train to Paris then on through the night to the Spanish Frontier. We changed trains and continued to Barcelona, arriving around midday. We had until evening to look around the beautiful Spanish city. Plenty to do and see in such a short time but there was another place in Barcelona that had to be seen. No, it wasn't that wonderful walk along famous Ramblas where someone who was abroad for the first time would be fascinated by the wonderful scene of marvellous shops, flowers and stalls selling absolutely everything.

No, it was off to the football ground at Nou Camp Stadium where the opening of the 1982 World Cup Finals took place. In 1960 it was brand new and was something really outside the world of football as I had known it in England.

My first view from the top of the stadium looking down towards the pitch was one I will always remember. Wembley was nothing compared with this. Little did I realise as I surveyed the scene that in a few years' time the team I was going to start in 1961 would be the hosts of this famous Club and the pennant presented at that time still hangs in their famous trophy room. Due to a pure coincidence the BBC filmed Terry Venables in this room whilst interviewing him for a special report on his recent success as manager of Barcelona.

They had won the Spanish First Division by a record number of points and English television, as always, likes to extol the success of an Englishman abroad. Lo and behold as the camera panned in on the wall there was the Grasmere pennant for all to see. I was quite proud to see this record of our visit still so prominently displayed. After a complete tour of the stadium we hurriedly made our way back to the Port where we were to catch the night boat to Majorca.

Two weeks on this beautiful Spanish island, which in those days was uncommercialised, was really tremendous. I had my first taste of watching football in a foreign country and was fascinated by the different atmosphere and excitement generated by the crowd. I would have plenty of experience of this in years to come as I travelled the world with Grasmere Rovers but this was a new facet of football and I liked what I saw.

2

In the beginning

U p until 1961 my interest in football was purely the professional scene with Manchester United my number one followed, very closely, by Stockport County. As a United supporter I was very lucky. My support followed them in the pre-Munich days when players like Roger Byrne, Duncan Edwards and Tommy Taylor were household names. The Busby Babes were one of the first English teams to enter the European Cup. They were such a tremendous all-round side and so many more honours would surely have followed if they had been allowed by fate to survive the Munich air crash.

I saw their last game in England before that fateful day in Munich. They travelled to play Arsenal and gave a scintillating performance in beating them 4-3. How many teams score 4 goals at Highbury? They then travelled to Yugoslavia to play Red Star Belgrade. It was on the way home at a stopover in Munich that the most tragic accident in sporting history occurred.

All Manchester was in tears and people stayed up all night to hear the news bulletins about the condition of the survivors in hospital. It was a traumatic period for football in this country and it was so difficult to understand that players who I had watched develop into a very special team were no more.

To be a Manchester United supporter in those days and the years to follow were eventful, exciting and successful.

One such game was that memorable second leg of the European

Cup at home to Athletico Bilbao of Spain, on February 6th, 1957. Home in those days for Manchester United was Maine Road and it was filled to capacity to witness a game that will live in the memory of everyone who was lucky to be present, for the rest of their lives.

United were 5-3 down after the first leg in Spain. Away goals did not count in those days so a clear three goal win was required to warrant further progress. I was lucky to get a seat and saw a performance from United that took your breath away. How the crowd roared as wave after wave of United attacks swamped a magnificent Spanish defence. How they groaned when David Pegg shot over. How they gasped as Bilbao fullback Canito headed a Pegg shot off the line.

Before half time United scored. Duncan Edwards picked up a loose ball. His shot struck defender Mauri and rebounded to Dennis Violett who gleefully shot hard into the net. The second half pounded with excitement. Violett again had the ball in the net but the linesman's flag intervened. A few minutes later Liam Whelan again had the ball in the net but again the goal was ruled out. This was unbearable. The crowd were in hysterics. Then came a second goal from Taylor that levelled the scores. The crowd continued to roar. Ten minutes to go, nine, eight, still United attacked. Still the crowd roared and still Bilbao defended as if their lives depended upon it. Seven, six, five minutes left. Then came the greatest moment I can remember in watching professional football.

Taylor dribbled past two defenders and put the ball back to Johnny Berry who running in shot past Spanish 'keeper Carmelo. I don't know who was more breathless, the players or the crowd! People were hugging each other and had tears of excitement in their eyes. There have been many similar games since where teams have come from behind, but this was the first one of its kind and this sort of excitement was a new experience. That was certainly a game that will live forever in the memory.

The only football in my mind in those days was professional football and Manchester United. Amateur football was never even thought of and least of all being involved in the running of such a side. I was also interested in collecting programmes from all over the world and I had built up quite a collection. It was a growing and popular hobby taking over from the traditional stamp collecting and train spotting. Collecting soccer programmes had given me many contacts with people who were also interested in swapping programmes.

One such person was Alan Grafton. In one letter he wrote to me he said: "Can my football team play your football team?" I was a little taken back as I didn't have a football team. My only football team was Manchester United and I'm sure Alan didn't mean a game against them. I wrote back politely to Alan and then dismissed the thought from my mind.

Alan Grafton was a leading administrator in local Manchester football. He had been a Secretary of a large Sunday League and in his playing days he was a terrific goalkeeper. He did a lot of work locally and became a JP before deservedly rewarded by receiving the OBE from the Queen.

It was December 1960 and on my way home from the office, I used to have a talk about football to the lads who lived in Grasmere Avenue. One of these lads was a youngster called Barrie Dean. We talked about United. He was intelligent and for a 14-year-old, very knowledgeable. He then came out with the question that in time was going to change my whole life.

"Why don't we start our own football team?" I didn't know what to say. I stood there for several minutes thinking about that question. Then just for something to say I said: "How do we do that?" Barry ignored the question. I don't think he knew the answer. Then he said: "You could be the manager".

The only manager I knew was Matt Busby! The thought appealed to me but it just didn't seem possible. I replied: "If you can find a team, I will manage them".

I continued home and never gave the conversation any more thought. That is until the following night. A knock came on our back door. I opened it to find Barrie Dean standing there with an excited look on his face. "I've got eleven players who want to play," he blurted out. I looked at him and realised very slowly what he was saying. Where do we find fixtures? What about a ground? I was at a complete loss as to what to do.

Then the letter from Alan Grafton became a lifeline. My team played his team on the 7th January, 1961 and Grasmere Rovers were born. This was the small beginning of something that became huge. A letter appeared in the local Football Green from someone called Derek Locke. He wanted to start a junior football League on Sundays and anyone interested was to attend a meeting. What a coincidence. What an opportunity. I attended the first meeting of the Manchester and District Sunday Football League. I became Minute and Press Secretary and Grasmere Rovers were founder members of a League and remained such until 1983.

Our first home was Cringle Fields, a Manchester muddy park pitch. We were an Under 16 team and I was a football team manager. I had as my assistant Bernard Tuson, a friend who used to accompany me to watch United. His brother John was the team captain. This all seemed like a good idea. I could watch United on Saturday and get involved with Grasmere on a Sunday.

We started our League fixtures in September 1961 but didn't set the world on fire. We had a young side and against some excellent teams we struggled to hold our own. It was a difficult season but I enjoyed it. I didn't think at this stage that Matt Busby should worry too much about his job!

As we approached the end of the season my wanderlust bug was saying we had to go on a close season tour. Nothing too exotic to start with - so we went to Blackpool, played a game then came home. Fantastic, we really enjoyed that. I never thought then that future journeys would cover over 300,000 miles to places all over the world. We had some good lads playing for us in those days. Frank Seymour was our stalwart centre-half. He was so reliable and gave us great service. He was a Director of William Hill's. Alwin Thompson was another superb player. A tricky left winger, he was also a ball boy at Old Trafford for United. He too is now a Director of several companies. Play for Grasmere Rovers and become a Director!

Meanwhile I was enjoying life as a committee member of the Manchester and District League. This position plus the job as a football manager gave me terrific experience for later in life as I pursued my career as a Stockbroker.

At the end of the following season we went on another close season tour when we travelled down to London for the weekend. We played one game, saw the Rugby League Cup Final at Wembley and really enjoyed being "on tour".

However, that yearning of always wanting to go abroad, particularly now I had my own football team, was forever in the foreground so I decided to make some enquiries on how to organise such a tour. I found a company who specialised in organising travel, together with football games, and I managed to get a party of sixteen to travel to Belgium and Holland.

We were on our way into Europe at last! A game was arranged in Belgium against VC Adelaars and along the coast in Holland against Groede. Our base in Belgium was the holiday town of Blankenburg. This was the general format of the trips I was to organise; a holiday and some good football games.

We travelled from Manchester by train and then boat from Dover to Ostend. I enjoyed the experience of again being in a foreign country. Then came our first set back. A telephone call was received from the travel company saying that our game against VC Adelaars had been called off due to the Belgium F.A. not giving permission for the game to be played. I couldn't believe it. Apparently, it was the close season and no way would the Belgium F.A. allow us to play the game.

This would rarely happen today because to play a game abroad every English club must apply to the Football Association for permission to play. The Football Association then informs the FA in the country in which the game is played.

What was I to do now? Here we were in a foreign country and after all that travelling by train and boat the game had been cancelled. I wasn't going to be beaten and was delighted when a game was arranged against the local soccer team Blankenburg. They were open age and we were only a junior team but it was a game. The match was played "behind closed doors" without the Belgium FA knowing anything about it - which probably was just as well - because this game created a score that may have gone into the Guinness Book of Records.

At Piccadilly station for our first ever trip abroad on our way to Belgium and Holland.

Our first game on foreign soil. Captain John Tuson (left) exchanges pennants with the Groede captain in Holland, 1963.

We lost the game 13-0 and in those days of wingers, Blankenburg had a luxury - two wingers! In fact, these two players scored all the thirteen goals between them, one scoring six and the other seven. They were magic and taught us a lesson that playing abroad against experienced sides is a lot more difficult than I imagined.

We moved on to Holland and to another defeat, this time only 8-0! A least we were improving but again we played a team much older and more experienced than ourselves. Was playing in Europe always going to be as difficult as this?

Despite the defeats, the lure of Europe lingered long after we had arrived home. I had to think of a new venue, somewhere exciting, somewhere that would be a challenge and something no amateur club had done before. My mind wandered back to that fantastic stadium in Barcelona. Dare I - should I - challenge them to a game?

My ambitious instincts answered very quickly. "Yes". I wrote to Club de Futbol, Barcelona on 27th November 1963 and received a reply on 12th December. To my astonishment they agreed to play their Youth team against Grasmere Rovers.

After recovering from the shock, I arranged that we stay at Lloret de Mar on the Costa Brava for two weeks and was thrilled that all the players jumped at the chance of playing such a game. I told a newspaper friend of mine, Stanley Browning, who sadly has since died, and on the following Sunday had every National newspaper in the country represented at Debdale Park to see our Manchester and District League game against Allison Villa.

Never has an amateur club playing on a Park pitch had such a following from the media. Reporters and photographers followed our every move in a 4-1 win and the Monday papers were full of the story that little Grasmere Rovers were going to play the millionaires of Spain in the mighty Barcelona Stadium. It was at this stage that I met, for the first time, Paul Hince.

Paul worked for the local newspaper and gave us a magnificent front page headline with two pictures on top of the page, under a heading saying, "From This, to This". The first picture was of a muddy goalmouth in Debdale Park and the second an aerial view of the magnificent Nou Camp Stadium.

Paul Hince went on to play professionally for Manchester City, Charlton Athletic, Bury and Crewe before going back to full time reporting with the Manchester Evening News. He was without doubt one of the best reporters on football I know. He made his reports interesting but always seemed to find an amusing angle in which to base his stories. As our League season finished and we started to prepare for our big game, training became an important part of the preparation. I decided to contact Henry Cockburn the former Manchester United and England wing half to supervise the training. Only the best for the best would do.

We had received a fantastic media response for the forthcoming game and people from all over the country wrote letters, some wishing us luck, one wishing to referee the match, another warning us not to go to a bullfight as he was waging a bloodless revolution in Spain. One wanted his son to be our mascot, but the strangest one of all came from a chap called Syd Smith of Covent Garden, London. He wrote saying that he was an ex-professional boxer and loved football. He was fascinated by Grasmere Rovers travelling to Spain and playing Barcelona in that wonderful stadium.

He said that he would re-organise his holiday so that he could be in Spain when we played the big game. He was so keen that when we arrived in Lloret de Mar he telephoned us at our hotel to arrange a meeting. We met on the beach and talked for many hours on boxing and football. He had fought at Madison Square Gardens in New York as a lightweight and his football love was West Ham United.

He came to watch us training at the local Lloret ground and seemed very interested in our preparation. I invited him to travel on our team coach to the game which he gladly accepted.

Our big day arrived, our team coach was waiting but no Syd Smith. We waited for half an hour. His hotel didn't know where he was. We went off without him and we haven't heard from Syd Smith to this day. He organised his holiday specially to see us play but when the day came he just vanished from the face of the earth. Life is full of unsolved mysteries!

The game against Barcelona was played in a temperature of 100° and everything was so different from playing on a muddy

Manchester Park pitch. Barcelona fielded 6 players who had played for Spain in the Junior World Cup Finals. Included in the side were two players who were to become full internationals and played such a big part in keeping Barcelona in the forefront of world soccer. They were Suares and Rexach.

We lined up against these multi-million all stars and after only five minutes the first goal was scored. Incredibly it wasn't Barcelona who scored it, but Grasmere Rovers. Dave Tennant put the ball into the net and the score read Barcelona 0 Grasmere Rovers 1. Study that score because it makes much more pleasant reading than the final result.

We continued to play well. The lads excelled themselves playing some superb football but the pace, the large pitch and that cruel hot sun were slowly making inroads into our performance. Barcelona struck and scored three goals after half an hour and although Wally Henderson pulled one back, we were suddenly chasing shadows.

At half time we were 5-2 down and as the players sank into the cool dressing rooms I searched for the secret remedy that lifts players and transforms them into a different team. I tried to remember the advice that Henry Cockburn had given us and also friendly tips offered by Roy Clarke and Dave Ewing who had experienced the Barcelona way of playing when turning out against them for Manchester City.

Half time stretched to over 15 minutes, the referee was urging us back on to the pitch. Must we take more punishment, or could we declare at half time? The players, like heroes decided that the show must go on and crawled back into action. Poor Alan Grafton thought he had an attack of lumbago as he continually went to pick the ball out of the back of the net. The final score of Barcelona 17 Grasmere Rovers 2 was a little unkind to say the least.

This was totally through inexperience of playing football abroad. The players had spent many hours sunbathing and had late nights. It is impossible to play a serious game of football and mix the pleasures of holidaying in a hot sun. This was a lesson we were to learn so often in the future!

That was the first big game of many we were to play in the future. Our pennant presented to Barcelona is still in their impressive trophy rooms proudly sharing our moment of glory with practically every top club in world soccer.

We made the long way home by train and boat. Another two and a half days travelling. It was as we were plodding through Central France and the scenery was becoming more and more boring that John Tuson said: "Why can't we fly when we go away next year?"

I looked at him in amazement. Flying certainly wasn't part of my vocabulary. I was literally frightened. The thought of it brought back memories of the Munich air crash. In fact, the thought of it simply terrified me.

The train bumped its way through France towards Paris. My back ached and the thought of three more hours from Paris to the coast plus a possible bumpy journey on the boat to Dover didn't make the journey any more pleasant. Added to that an hour and a half to London plus another four hours from London to Manchester made me think that there might be something in what John was saying after all. We had already been travelling a day and the thought that a flight would only take two hours began to appear slightly tempting.

Jumping for joy in the mud at Debdale Park after finding out that we are going to play the mighty Barcelona. Amongst others are: Peter O'Dwyer, goalkeeper Clifford Simpson, Eddie Lewis, Alan Rawcliffe and Frank Seymour.

3

To fly or not to fly

G rasmere Rovers were now beginning to make progress and were gradually making an impact on local soccer in Manchester. We appointed a President to the Club and were pleased to have Jimmy Cumbes in that position.

I had first met Jim in 1958 as I travelled down by train to the Manchester United and Bolton Cup Final. I was collecting train numbers - what a great hobby that was and Jim sat down in a spare seat opposite. He too was keen on train spotting and when we found that our tickets were for the same part of the ground, we stayed together and our friendship was formed.

Jimmy Cumbes went on to be a duel success at the top of the tree in football and cricket. He was goalkeeper for Tranmere Rovers, West Bromwich Albion and Aston Villa plus several other sides later in his career. He played at Wembley for Villa in their League Cup Final victory over Norwich.

In cricket he created a record by playing for four different counties where he went on to become General Manager at Warwickshire and Lancashire.

A great all-round sportsman is Jim and we were proud to have him as our President. He once had his own programme on local radio in Birmingham and put as much into the game as he got out of it. I was enjoying my work on the committee of the Manchester and District League. Every year we had Inter League games for each Division and thinking back it is amazing the players who have represented the League before they made it with a Football League Club.

One such player was Stan Bowles. He played as a left winger for Broadhurst Lads, a very efficient club run by Albert Booth. Stan played for the League side but we didn't think he played too well, so we dropped him for the next match! Paul Hart, David Cross, Len Cantello, Tony Brown, Tony Towers, Keith Hanvey, Gary Pierce, Ged Keegan and latterly Wayne Harrison, were other players who started in the Manchester and District League and moved on to greater pastures.

Another year was quickly passing by and it didn't seem long since we returned from Spain that plans were being made for another soccer holiday. We had to go somewhere different than Spain so the choice was Italy. Our base was to be Lido di Jesolo on the Adriatic and close to Venice.

The big question was how to get there. I thought of John Tuson's words of wisdom that we should go by air. I thought of that long journey by boat and train. I didn't really fancy that again, so I decided to compromise. We would travel by air from Manchester to Ostend in Belgium and then by motor coach right through Belgium into Luxembourg, Germany and through Switzerland before entering Italy.

I didn't relish the thought of flying but at least it would only take one hour to Ostend rather than one day, but I really looked forward to the travelling through so many countries. As it turned out, all that was in exact reverse.

My very first flight - and I really had butterflies as we waited at Manchester's Ringway Airport. The date was 22nd August 1965 and the aircraft was a small propeller Ambassador of Dan Air. Not exactly the most comfortable of aircraft to fill anyone with confidence.

I sat in the seat next to the gangway and must have spent the whole journey looking down at the floor. I didn't enjoy it one little bit but I had to admit that it was better than I had anticipated.

We then transferred to a motor coach and proceeded to travel for the rest of the day, through the night and the following day before we arrived in Jesolo, Italy. It was an interesting journey and we

Before our game with Jesolo in 1964

saw some new places such as Brussels, Lucerne and Milan, but the one disappointment was the travelling through Switzerland. From North to the South of the country it never stopped raining although it didn't hide the beautiful and exciting scenery that makes Switzerland somewhere very special.

We arrived in Lido di Jesolo and contact was made with the local football club. Jesolo FC were a semi-professional side, not of the standard of Barcelona, so we were hoping to do a lot better. They were very keen and during talks with their President he made a suggestion that has stuck with us until this very day.

"Can we call you Manchester AFC" he said.

The thought sounded exciting. Nobody abroad had heard of Grasmere Rovers and as long as people were not mixing us up with Manchester City or United, then there shouldn't be any problems.

I immediately agreed and thousands of posters were printed with 'Jesolo FC v Manchester AFC (inc. Grasmere Rovers)'. We now affiliate to the Manchester County FA as Manchester AFC and are known throughout the world.

The ground at Jesolo was nothing like Barcelona, but it was exciting as we prepared for the match. The game was to be refereed by Diego de Leo who was a FIFA referee from Mexico who was on holiday in Jesolo at the time. That really gave the game a sense of occasion with a Central American FIFA Referee officiating.

There were over 1,000 people in the ground, the biggest crowd up to that time we had played before. Captain was Jon de Pledge. Jon was captain of Manchester, not Jesolo! Jon was a good friend of mine, keen and very loyal. He was a photographer and he took some fantastic photographs.

I will never forget his face when he went to the centre circle to toss up and was handed the biggest bouquet of flowers I have ever seen. The game turned out to be rather one- sided again, although we only lost 8-0! The team we took wasn't as strong as the previous year, but again we were playing a side much more experienced than ourselves.

We visited Venice and it is now one of my favourite places. It has an atmosphere so different from anywhere else I have ever visited. St. Mark's Square was tremendous. Listening to the music and watching the people go by in front of St. Marks Church makes you forget the exorbitant price you pay for a cup of coffee and a cake!

A trip on a gondola is again something that was a new experience. It was like gliding down a main road full of water and turning left into a side street; the gondolier was singing his best Italian. Yes, a little different from a taxi ride through Manchester.

What a crying shame that Venice is slowly sinking and deteriorating. I only hope someone can find a solution to keep that great old City alive.

We made the long way back by coach. Amazingly the journey back through Switzerland met the same weather as before - rain. For the first time in my life I really looked forward to reaching Ostend airport and the flight back to Manchester. Two days on a coach bumping around Europe and the previous years' experience of travelling back from Spain finally took its toll. The time had arrived when I actually wanted to fly in an aeroplane.

To think that it would only take one hour to get back home was making me believe that perhaps flying was a good thing after all. As we touched down in Manchester I was finally convinced that if I wanted to conquer the world the only way that I could do it was to travel everywhere by plane.

I had organised three overseas trips for Grasmere Rover and despite our heavy defeats I had the adrenalin flowing with organising these footballing holidays. One great thing about them is meeting and getting to know all kinds of people.

The one thing that football has taught me is how everyone is different. A typical example is a football changing room. You look around and see 15 lads: some are quiet and hardly speak a word, others say too much, whilst there are cheeky ones and polite ones. The same of course goes for all walks of life, but that football changing room epitomises people.

I have made many great friends from football. Someone who I have known all my life - literally is Graham Clifford. We were born in the same maternity ward, went to school together and during the first season of Grasmere he joined the team and has given great service to the Club.

Someone who has been on most of our overseas tours is Keith Bateman. He had a painting and decorating shop in Hale and we spent many hours together travelling the world. Sadly, Keith died in 2013 after a long illness; he will be sorely missed.

Another year was going by and there was a further trip to organise. Wherever it was we just had to fly ALL the way. Again, it was somewhere different, Northern Portugal and a place called Povoa de Varzim, a coastal resort just south of Oporto. We went by plane all the way from Manchester to Oporto, what a great way to travel!

I enjoyed the flight, that is until we landed in Oporto. It was dark but we didn't realise until we landed that it was foggy. We learnt in the airport lounge that the pilot had been given a choice of either landing in the fog or going an extra 450 miles on to Lisbon. He had decided to risk landing in Oporto. I couldn't believe it.

That particular aircraft must have been fated because two years later it crashed in Stockport killing everyone on board. Keith Kushner, a member of our party on the Portugal trip, had taken the aircraft number and it corresponded to the one that came down.

It gives you a sickening feeling when coincidences like this happen. We had been allowed into the cockpit on the Portugal flight and in those days I had never heard of a plane flying on automatic pilot. I couldn't believe it when I saw the pilot sitting there eating his dinner, apparently oblivious to what was happening around him. It was an even bigger shock later when he walked casually down the length of the aircraft. Such modern flying techniques were unknown to me in those days.

We had one game organised in Pontevedra which was situated in Northern Spain and this turned out to be a fantastic experience. Pontevedra were then in the Spanish First Division and we were to play their Youth team. We were still a young side so it was obviously going to be hard game.

On arrival in Pontevedra we were taken to a restaurant in the mountains and treated to a magnificent meal. What a great preparation before a big game, a heavy meal and a tour around the town!

There were more than 2,000 people in the magnificent stadium and we really felt in the big time. A cup had been put up for the winners and another for the losers. This was one game we just couldn't lose. Well we did really, as the meal, tiredness and a superior side beat us 8-2. Another walloping but as Peter Coster held up the cup it was a worthwhile exercise. The Pontevedra club proved great hosts as they took us back into the mountains for another great feast.

Povoa de Varzim was one of those resorts where you thought in a few years' time it would develop into one of the major resorts in Europe. Surprisingly you never hear of the place now. Presumably the lack of money in that area has been a major problem.

One day Keith Bateman and I decided to hire bikes and go for a ride up the coast. It was to lead to the strangest way I have ever organised a football match. We battled up the coast road against a gale force wind and we decided to make our way back inland where it was slightly calmer. Suddenly we came upon a large wall where there were hundreds of bikes parked. On investigating we found ourselves outside a small football ground.

A few hundred people were watching a game between two young sides on a pitch of hard sand. What a great chance of organising another game against a team of players our age. We found the secretary and within minutes a game had been organised for the following day.

We were asked as to what time we wanted the kick off. Every day we had been in Povoa it had started cool and misty but by midday the sun had become very hot. The answer was to kick off in the morning whilst it was still cool.

The following morning, we made the short journey to the ground and couldn't believe it when it turned out to be the hottest morning of the holiday. The sun reflected off the white sand pitch and it was difficult to keep your eyes open never mind play football. We lost 5-1 but were grateful for the game and another experience. The team was called Rio Ave and, in those days, they were a small team playing in a local Portuguese League. Now they are a big club and play in the Portuguese First Division alongside Benfica. How times can change in football.

One of the players on the Portugal trip was John McArdle known as the Duke. He went on to make 593 appearances for Grasmere Rovers and was one of the best clubmen we have ever had. There are not many players who play that number of games for one club.

4

A meeting with Di Stefano

It was now 1967 and time for another trip. Today Benidorm doesn't sound particularly attractive but in those days it was somewhere new and exciting. Grasmere as a team was improving and we had signed some good players. Most of them made this trip and we had probably the best team so far taken abroad.

I wrote to Elche, another Spanish First Division Club, and requested a game against their youth side. They accepted and we were about to play the most exciting game we have ever had on foreign soil. Other games were arranged against Villajoyosa and Alcoy.

Villajoyosa came first and their open age side faced us on their hard sand pitch. Before the game captain Billy Headland was introduced to the local beauty queen. In those days we had a different captain for every game as they always received the best treatment. We lost the match 3-2 but we gave them an excellent game before 2,000 people. Notice the improvement in our result!

We were ready for the big one. The local press visited our hotel for interviews. We were really in the big time now. The previous year in 1966 England had won the World Cup at Wembley and any team from England was an attraction

The Manager of Elche at that time was the legendary Alfredo di Stefano. He was one of the greatest players the world has ever known. His deep lying centre forward role for the great

Real Madrid was something the world of soccer will always remember. Players of his calibre don't grow on trees and my one hope was that we would get the opportunity to meet him.

Elche is famous for its dates - the kind you eat! - and we had a short pre-match tour of some date palms. We arrived at the ground one hour before the scheduled time of kick off and had a good look around the ground that played host to several World Cup games in 1982. We prepared for the game. At 6.45 p.m. I started my pre-match talk to the players, working hard to get them wound up. Reminding them that this was the most important game they had ever played.

We could hear the clatter above as the crowd settled into their seats. "Right lads, let's go and show them how good English soccer is." With those words the dressing room door opened and in stepped a Spanish official to tell us in his best English that the kick off had been put back one hour!

I was flabbergasted! Just as the players were all prepared for battle we were stopped in our tracks from going into action. Apparently, the kick off time had been wrongly advertised as 8.00 p.m. and we had to wait for the entire crowd to arrive. Another typical example of gross inefficiency. Anything to put the visitors off and give the home team a psychological advantage.

The players kicked their heels, my team talk was in ruins and we would have to start all over again. Then came one of the greatest moments in my life. The door opened and in walked Di Stefano. The King himself. He looked majestic as he strode over to me and shook hands. It was a very proud moment. He then shook hands with every member of the team. That is something all of us will remember for the rest of our lives.

For several days I had been worried about how well or badly we would perform. We had suffered some big defeats in the past few years but I was very concerned that we didn't get a hammering in this game.

There were 5,000 people in the Altebix stadium and the atmosphere as we walked out was electric. This was our first game under floodlights and the butterflies were fluttering as we kicked off. Elche moved the ball around well - very well - but we appeared to be containing them. They had an inside forward who looked useful. At 18 years old he was already in the first team playing against all the top sides in Spain.

His name was Asensi and two years later he was to be transferred to Barcelona. He went on to play many times for Spain and in the 1978 World Cup Finals in Argentina he was the Spanish captain.

Half time approached and the score sheet was still blank. We had had a great first half. I was already feeling elated. Could we keep it up? The players looked good. Although it was now nearly 10.00 p.m. it was still very warm but unlike the Barcelona game we were better prepared and the players had that little extra ability and determination.

Four minutes into the second half we scored. A shot from John Rogan was too hot for the goalkeeper to handle and Mike Cuerden, following up, hit the back of the net. What a tremendous feeling that was.

The game continued and the second half appeared to last three hours. Elche attacked and attacked but didn't we tackle well? Perhaps too well and at times as we got a little desperate.

There were still 25 minutes to go when one particular tackle from Paul Fitzgerald didn't endear himself to the Spanish crowd. They threw stones and cushions onto the pitch and when John Rogan stood facing the crowd like a conductor of the Halle Orchestra, the referee immediately sent him off.

The match report later said "I sent Rogan off for inciting the crowd." We were down to ten men but that wasn't the last of our handicaps. Our goalkeeper Barry Broadbent who up to this time had performed heroics to defy the Spanish forwards, twisted his ankle. We didn't have a reserve keeper so Barry had to stay on hobbling around. Barry was a hero, he always had been. He was one of the best goalkeepers we have ever had.

The minutes ticked agonisingly away. I looked at my watch every 15 seconds. We were holding on desperately. The crowd that earlier had been hostile were now cheering on their team. I was sitting on the grass behind the goal that Barry was guarding on one leg. The referee had played three minutes over time. I was convinced he was waiting for Elche to score.

I was shouting at the referee to blow his whistle. He ignored me and the waves of Elche's white and green shirts continued to rain down on our goal. Now you wonder why managers don't suffer from more heart attacks.

Then it was all over. Without doubt one of our best ever victories on foreign soil. It was our first too. Everything had been against us from the start but we had fought against all the odds to win a game we didn't honestly think was possible. This was the moment I had dreamed of ever since I had ideas of taking a team abroad. It was worth every minute it had taken to organise.

Elche were tremendous hosts and took us out for a feast that was even more enjoyable after winning the game. The final accolade was in the morning papers when the match report gave us a tremendous write up.

One comment said "In summing up we consider that the Manchester side came well prepared and played characteristically in the same pattern as the English side that won the World Cup."

For an amateur side, that was a glowing report and we felt proud to be furthering the cause of English football. Full marks to all the players who had played in that game, they were all tremendous.

One of the stars in that match was fullback Roger Dilkes. He played many years for Grasmere and was always a credit to the game. It therefore came as a shock one day when he said to me. "I'm going to finish playing football and take up refereeing. I reckon I can go further as a referee than I can as a player." I didn't argue with Roger, he usually spoke a lot of sense but I thought he would be a loss to the amateur game.

Roger became a Premier League referee and was one of the best in the country – a well deserved accolade!

Another player I signed with Roger Dilkes was Ian Halfpenny. What a good player he was. He was a big strapping centre half who used to say when under pressure, "put snow on it." He played in the Huddersfield Town Reserve side but one thing stopped him from making any further progress as a footballer — studying to be an accountant. Ian spent almost every night of the week studying - which must have tested the patience of his girlfriend Heather - who later became his wife. However, that patience paid off as Ian became a Partner in his own accountancy firm.

Tragically, Ian died suddenly at a young age many years ago, leaving Heather with two sons. Some years later Heather moved to Wisconsin, America, where she now lives with her second husband Robert.

Our final game on this Benidorm trip was up in the mountains of the Sierra Nevada where the film 'El Cid' was made. We played Alcoy without a recognised goalkeeper - as Barry was still injured - and before the biggest crowd yet of 7,000 we went down 12-0 to a much more experienced Spanish Third Division side.

It had been a good trip but that final result did not hide the excitement of our first overseas victory playing under such trying conditions. We would still look forward to the following year.

That was to the place I had first visited as an overawed youngster — Majorca. The feature of this trip was that the four games were played on completely different surfaces. The first was in the stadium of Athletico Baleares which was beautiful grass.

The second was on the bone hard sand pitch of Lluchmayor where we were beaten by a disputed free kick. The third was in the beautiful coastal resort of Pollensa where the football pitch was just like the beach.

Finally, we travelled through the mountains into Soller where a last-minute goal saw us defeated 2-1 on a pitch full of stones. Over 1,000 people were crammed into the ground and the mountain backdrop gave the game a very special setting.

On all our trips abroad, we have a mixed party of footballers, girlfriends, wives, partners and supporters. On this trip to Majorca Roger Dilkes invited Jean Harper (née Taylor) who was a popular, friendly girl and when she finally went to live first in Coventry and then Brighton she kept in touch with everyone back home. Jean has been a big part of the Grasmere scene. She used to bring half time drinks for the players and served on the Manchester and District Committee for a time as Minute

Secretary. Football is full of these unsung heroes.

Majorca is a beautiful island although now very spoilt by the holiday traffic. It has so many contrasts and the capital, Palma, is a superb place.

We now had a good side at Grasmere and in the under 21 age group we started to win trophies. All those defeats in the early years were now beginning to be worthwhile as winning was becoming a habit.

I thought the time was right to go back to Lloret de Mar. I had liked Lloret, a compact resort with plenty to do and lots of places to visit nearby. Again, I arranged four games and with the good players we now had in the team, we were full of confidence in taking on anyone who wanted a game.

On our previous visit to Lloret I had met a chap called Emanuel Weiss who was an ex Hungarian International who had played in Czechoslovakia for Slovan Bratislava. He had helped to coach us and acted as our interpreter. The only problem when you have an interpreter is that you don't know what they are really saying when they are speaking to the opposition. Mr. Wiess will enter this story again later.

Our first game was in a place called Blanes and we had a tremendous game before 2,000 people and a very fair 2-2 draw. Our goalkeeper on this trip was a slightly built lad called Eric Bates. If ever anyone gave a false impression it was Eric, for what he lacked in size he made up for in agility and guts. In this game against Blanes he gave one of the best exhibitions of goalkeeping I have ever seen. At the end of the match he was clapped off the field by the whole crowd and both teams lined up for him in a very emotional tribute to a superb performance.

Our next game produced our biggest win so far when we beat Malgrat 8-1. A 2-2 draw with Calella meant that we were undefeated in our first three games. Things were looking up.

The big game against CF Lloret in the place where we were staying was saved until last and what a big game it turned out to be. Our friend Mr Wiess had been acting as the go between and I quickly realised what he had been telling the officials at Lloret. We went out to find the whole town covered with posters advertising our game, but instead of Manchester AFC it said Manchester United!

I am usually a fairly calm kind of person but this time I went berserk. I quickly went to find the Lloret officials and demanded that the posters were taken down immediately and reprinted with our proper name. At first, they weren't too keen but when I told them that we would not play the game they soon jumped into action.

A day later new posters adorned all the bars and the game was quickly on again. When I confronted Mr. Wiess he just gave a shrug of his shoulders as though he didn't know anything about it.

All these fixtures that we play abroad are for the love of the game and most of all to give experience of playing in a foreign country to the players who take part. We never ask for any money although we demand transport between our hotel and the ground. Anything else we receive is counted as a bonus.

My friend Mr. Wiess and the Spanish officials obviously saw a great opportunity of making some money by advertising that Manchester United were in town. The last thing we want is to be confused with our professional counterparts.

I have never seen so many posters advertising a game. Every window in every shop advertised the "friendly international". The kick off was 10.00pm and although by this time I was fairly experienced in preparing for a match on foreign soil, the old butterflies were there again and I sensed something a little more special about this game.

We arrived at the ground around 9.00pm and my fears were realised. We could hardly get into the ground as people surrounded the little stadium. My mind went back to those posters advertising Manchester United. Would all these people expect to be seeing Bobby Charlton, Denis Law and George Best?

My bottle was really going now. We locked ourselves into the confines of our small dressing room. It wasn't our fault if everybody expected to see Manchester United. We had had all those posters torn down and our own name correctly advertised.

At 9.50pm I was given the honour of leading the teams onto the field. We went through a dark tunnel and there was only room for us to walk in single file. Suddenly, I emerged into the open and the glare of the floodlights was like the turning on of a switch as the crowd broke into a nerve-shattering roar. The tunnel was by the corner flag and as I led the team nervously to the centre circle, I glanced around to witness people everywhere.

The ground was full, the gates were closed. People hung on branches in trees surrounding the ground. A large hotel behind one goal must have been charging admittance to watch the game from the balconies. Although there were officially only 3,000 people present, it was a new ground record for the Lloret club and the tiny ground was bursting at the seams.

Well, I always said that my idea of taking amateur footballers abroad was to give them a taste of what it is like to play abroad in front of a crowd. Certainly, these lads were given a taste of excitement and an experience they will always remember.

We performed well and despite going down 3-1 gave a good display under the conditions. Our goal was scored by Ken Tidmas who had had a great tour scoring five goals. I was pleased that we didn't get any comeback from the crowd regarding our name and apparently people on holiday and the locals were just pleased to attend a football game. Certainly, I was very relieved afterwards.

It is amazing the stories that come out of football after the event; things that nobody knows about at the time. One such story concerned our goalkeeper Eric Bates. He was our hero on this trip, but a few days before the Lloret game he told me he couldn't play. I thought he was joking but he said that he couldn't see properly at night under floodlights.

That was a frightening situation to be in. A big game coming up, only one goalkeeper in the party and here we were with a goalkeeper who couldn't see! Eric wore contact lenses and it took hours of persuasion to convince him that it would be better for the team with a goalkeeper who couldn't see than one who wasn't used to being a goalkeeper. Under the circumstances he did well but apparently, he couldn't see most of the shots until they were almost upon him.

Football is full of little anecdotes, most of which the public never hear about. I remember a game we played abroad one year when a member of the party - a non-player I might add, caused us all kinds of problems. The party was in uproar and we couldn't have had a worse preparation for a big game, or so we thought. The team went out to make a mockery of the pre-match planning by putting up a fantastic performance and finishing 3-0 winners. If only the crowd had known that we had so many major problems before the game.

It probably goes to show that the most organised of pre-match planning doesn't always win games. The most important part of the game is what goes on during those 90 minutes on the field not the 90 minutes before the game.

Probably our best ever Grasmere side from 1967. All of them remain great friends today.

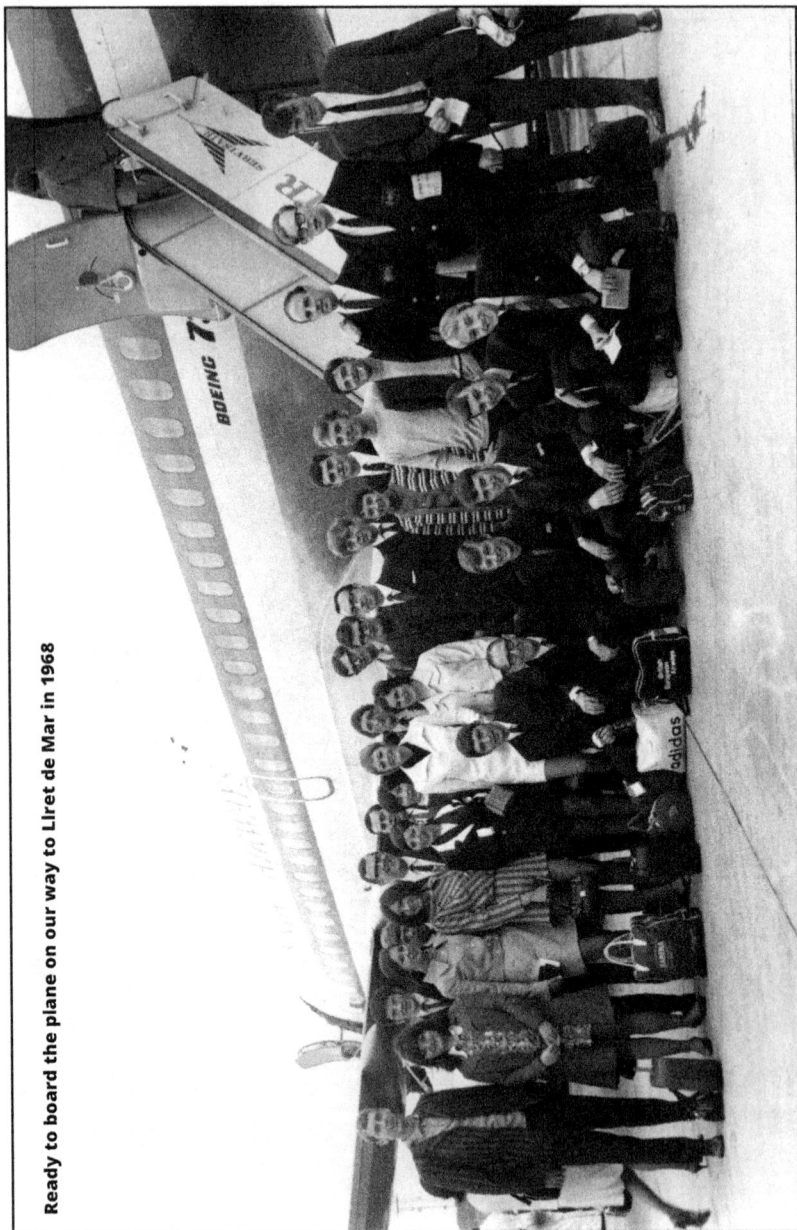

Ready to board the plane on our way to Llret de Mar in 1968

5

Behind the Iron Curtain

B y this time, 1970, it was becoming the normal thing to organise an overseas footballing holiday. We used to travel in August just before our season at home started. I would start planning the trip in October and spend the next ten months writing to teams and promoting the holiday amongst members of our club.

Each person on the holidays pays his own way so if a member of the club couldn't afford to go, then it was unfortunate. That is why the strength of the sides varies so much every year. The system I use is to first of all find a suitable place, usually somewhere on the coast. Travelling to the resort is important. It is no use going somewhere that takes hours to get to from the airport. The hotel is also important, all the time thinking of cost and trying to keep the price down as much as possible, but at the same time trying not to lower standards.

When a good combination of flight and hotel has been chosen, then the football side can be organised. Every country in the world plays soccer and as I will explain later, most of them are good at it. Even the so called unknown footballing countries are now raising their standards and there are no easy touches especially when the game is being played on foreign soil.

There are many ways to organise football abroad. Several companies organise the whole thing, travel, hotel and football. I have rarely gone through these companies as they specialise usually in Belgium, Holland and France. They are however an excellent way of tasting the delights of a soccer holiday.

Another way to organise the football side is to write to the Football Association of the country you are visiting and ask to be put in touch with the standard of team you require. This can be very difficult because standards overseas differ so much from ours.

In England we have every possible standard from our Premier Division right down to the lowest amateur game on the park. A player has no problem in finding his level although many think they are better than they really are. Or you find the better player who plays in a lower standard so that he can help his club to win trophies.

Generally, on the continent and taking Spain as an example, there is no gradual sliding scale. After the National First and Second Divisions we come to a very large regional Third Division. These are followed by the 'First Amateur Leagues' which are of a standard probably on a par to the new North West Counties League and then to find the lesser standards, the grounds suddenly change from grass to all kinds of gravel, sand and stone.

Before today I have written to the "Futbol Club" in the town where we were staying presuming that they had a football team and hoping for a reply. This worked several times although the standard of the sides has varied considerably.

I receive many telephone calls from people who want advice on how to organise a football trip abroad, on average about one a week. First of all, find out the maximum amount of money that the players wish to spend and make sure they are keen. I've heard of so many people who have started to organise something only to cancel the trip because of a sudden lack of interest.

Study the holiday package brochures where a good idea on place and price can be gained and when you have found somewhere you want to go then at least the flight and hotel can be taken care of by the travel agent and basically the organiser can get down to organising the football side of the trip. It can be very exciting but always be prepared for the person who cancels, sometimes at the last moment.

I was getting a little tired of Spain and Italy and felt the desire and ambition to go somewhere different. I scoured the holiday brochures and found something entirely different for only a little more in price - Romania. A trip behind the Iron Curtain appealed and it must have done within the club because it attracted 40 people, the most I have ever taken abroad. Usually we average around 30 people but I had to close this one before it became unmanageable.

My old "friend" Emanuel Wiess was enquiring where we were going that year and the worst thing I did was to tell him. We were travelling from Gatwick and Mr. Wiess who now lived in London was to meet us at the airport.

As I stood in the lounge with my friend Keith Young I said to Keith, "I wonder what the chances are of old Wiess missing the plane."

"Hello Mr. Davies, how are you", said a familiar voice from behind me. Keith just turned away laughing as Wiess joyously joined our party and proceeded to mither the life out of me. The aircraft we were travelling on to Constanta in Romania was an old Tupalev Prop jet and during the whole four-hour journey I had Mr. Wiess talking into my left ear. The noise of the aircraft engines was so loud that I honestly couldn't understand a word he was talking about.

I shouldn't really be so unkind to Mr. Wiess, he meant well, but why did he have to follow us on these trips?

The Hotel Flora had been overbooked and we were switched to the Piccadilly. Not a common problem but fancy going all the way to Rumania and finding yourself staying at the Hotel Piccadilly.

I liked Mamaia, it had a beautiful beach and there was plenty of greenery. All the hedges had flowers and the appearance of the place looked so different from that of a communist resort. The people, however, looked very drab, no colour and it was difficult to buy decent clothes. Most of us received offers for various clothing and we could have sold items for double the cost we paid for them originally.

One other problem in Romania is that they think nothing of

serving the food cold. In the hotel restaurant they would bring a large urn of soup and if you were lucky to be in from the start the soup would be reasonably hot. That same soup, however, was kept in the restaurant and if you came in half an hour later then you were unlucky, it would be served cold.

Egg and chips was quite a common dish but they thought nothing of serving it to you cold. If you told them to take it back and warm it up, they would look at you with a blank stare. If you were in a hurry to get out, forget it. A meal could take over three hours to serve.

Our first game was in Constanta against a Romanian Second Division club and we did well to only lose 3-0. One of the problems, as I have mentioned before, is the different interpretation of referees overseas. We used to always encourage players to talk to each other on the field. After only two minutes in this game Doug Welsh shouted to his mate Ernie Kerridge for the ball and couldn't understand when the referee gave a blast on his whistle giving a free kick against him. Doug stood glaring at the referee, hands on hips. If only looks could kill! The referee glared back and put his hand to his mouth, saying something in Romanian that presumably meant, keep your mouth shut.

Now saying that to Doug was really inappropriate because Dougie was always talking. I'm sure he talked in his sleep, but to be fair Doug always spoke sense. He was a great lad and a useful footballer too. Another player who gave us great service.

Ernie Kerridge was another character, known as "Freezer" because he worked for a freezer company - sounds natural enough. Ernie scored a lot of goals, but the thing that always amazed me about him was that I've never seen anyone eat so much in all my life, and he never put on weight. If you enjoyed your food it was dangerous to sit on the same table as Ernie. He made you nervous watching everything you ate and always hoping that you might leave something.

I had organised our second game in Bulgaria. One of their officials travelled up to our hotel and we had three-way talks, him, me and Mr. Wiess. Or should we say two way talks as the official from Spartac Varna and Mr. Wiess discussed the various aspects of the game in Bulgarian!

Occasionally Mr. Wiess would say to me, "Do you think we should do this." I would answer "Yes" and the two of them would rattle on with me as anything but an avid listener. This continued for almost two hours and I don't think I had contributed more than a dozen words. Mr. Wiess was a big help as an interpreter, but I would like to have known a little more of what was going on.

Even so, the day we had in Varna, Bulgaria, was one of the best we have ever spent. Spartac Varna were top of the Bulgarian Second Division and they sent a coach to transport us the 90 miles to the second city in Bulgaria. They first of all took us to the beautiful seaside resort of Golden Sands and to a hotel on a cliff with a marvellous view of the beach.

We relaxed in the hotel in true professional style before making our way to the stadium. When we arrived in our dressing room I have never seen such a feast that lay before us. There was every conceivable soft drink, rows upon rows of fresh fruit and boxes with all kinds of chocolates. I wouldn't let the players be tempted before the game but I'm sure everyone who knows me will know that you didn't have to ask me twice.

The game was a grand affair with 7,000 people present and another occasion when flowers were presented to us before the game. Unfortunately, we had to leave Ian Halfpenny behind in Romania and his loss from the side was apparent as we struggled to a 6-0 defeat. Not too bad a result when one considers that the same Varna side moved up the following season into the Bulgarian First Division and in 1984 played Manchester United in the UEFA Cup.

After the game we went back to the hotel in Golden Sands for a marvellous meal. Despite the result we had an enjoyable day and there is nothing wrong with the hospitality of teams from behind the Iron Curtain.

This trip to Romania gave me an opportunity I just couldn't miss. There were several day trips available from Constanta and one was to Kiev in Ukraine. Ten years earlier I had looked forward to my first ever visit abroad to see that magic coast line of France and then put a first giant step on foreign soil to fulfil a treasured dream. In those ten years since that eventful day I had fulfilled many dreams of seeing some wonderful places.

On the 11th September, 1970 I paid £16 17s 6d. for a day trip to Kiev. I was as excited as if it were my first time abroad. I had tried to get some football organised for us in Ukraine, but I wasn't as experienced in those days as I am now. Just nine of us made the two-hour flight to Kiev; then an organised coach tour around the impressive city. Again, it was surprising to see the number of parks and attractive buildings, but again it was the inhabitants who looked so utterly miserable.

We were only taken to places that they wanted us to see and when we made efforts to walk away from our parked coach, the courier would immediately put a stop to that. I enjoyed Kiev. It was a new world to me and another country on the map ticked off.

On every trip since Benidorm in 1967 I have taken a cine film and recorded highlights of the holiday. It produces a wonderful record of all the places we have visited and proof of all the games that have been staged.

Some members in our party to Kiev got the wind up when I photographed fighter aircraft at the side of the airport. Keith Bateman thought we may get arrested but the film is still intact and there for all to see.

The party we took to Romania was our biggest ever at 40, but only 38 returned on the flight to England. Wally Roberts and Dougie Welsh had other ideas.

For some incredible reason these two lads decided to hitch hike back to England. For anyone to decide to take the high road and the low road back home was beyond comprehension, especially for two intelligent people like they were.

Dougie takes up the story:

"Maybe I was thinking of the bumpy journey from England that Roger Dilkes had described as like being at a rock concert without any music!

It seems fairly straightforward to hitch hike from Romania

into Bulgaria, Greece, Italy, France and then home to England; looking at a map it appeared even more so. However, thinking about it now we must have been totally mad!

I had been a Boy Scout as a youngster, staying at various hostels, and thought there would be loads of these resting places in Europe.

Before we left Romania we stuffed as much food as we could into our bags – and the rest of the party waved us goodbye.

We walked towards Bulgaria. Naturally the main part of hitch hiking is to hail lifts from passing traffic, but two hours later we were still walking with little sign of any.

Eventually we reached the border and after a long wait and scrutiny from the guards we were allowed through.

Minutes later a lorry stopped to offer us our first lift and we wearily climbed aboard and sat back to enjoy the journey. It was only when the driver was asking us whether we had any money that we realised he wanted paying. Wally scrambled into the back of the lorry as talking about money wasn't one of his favourite topics.

With only about five miles behind us, the driver told us to get out of the vehicle. However, it wasn't long before a 'posh' car pulled up alongside us and the friendly English-speaking driver took us to a hostel in Varna.

Unfortunately, there were no rooms available so we decided to walk three miles to the Golden Sands beach. It seemed ideal: chairs and tables to turn into beds, but when we heard voices and saw police and soldiers walking towards us we quickly did a disappearing act. That was the end of that little idea!

By this time the food in our bag was getting rather stale. "Let's give up" said Wally, which seemed like an excellent idea.

We made our way to Varna airport which was another five mile hike, but there were no flights to the UK. We had no alternative but to sleep at the airport which certainly wasn't the best night's rest we had had.

Next stop was the railway station and we boarded a train bound for the capital, Sofia. We badly needed help and advice so the idea was to make our way to the Embassy.

We were so weary after another five hour journey. It was slow and packed with peasants who had baskets of fruit around their waists.

Suddenly the train came to a juddering halt. All of the lights went out and the fruit went in all directions around the carriage. It was absolute chaos as people were shouting and trying to restore some semblance of order.

Unashamedly we grabbed a melon and felt our hunger and thirst disappear as we tucked in. Even Wally was smiling!

The British Embassy was so helpful and we were told that we had enough money to return to England by train.

Never has it been so good to arrive home and never, ever will I go hitch hiking again!"

6

Tournament tantrums

After our trip behind the Iron Curtain we came back to normality the following year with a trip to Cattolica in Italy. Every year we attracted new people to our touring scene and I'm pleased to say that most of them are great people. This was a particularly good one meeting for the first-time people like Ricky Green, Peter Healey and Eddie Cuncar.

One person who was making his first trip was one of the best-known people in Manchester amateur soccer, Roy Davies. At that time, he was coming towards the end of a very illustrious career as a goalkeeper. Roy, in his early thirties, sported white hair and a black moustache so he was easily recognised. He gave us many years' service as a player and was our first team coach, a job that he did with the same enthusiasm that has always been his trademark.

We had three matches on this trip to Italy. The first was against the local side Cattolica which we lost 2-1 in temperatures of 104°. For the second game we travelled up to the Republic of San Marino. Now that really is a beautiful place. People who are fortunate enough to live there don't pay any income tax being one of those tax-free havens of which we would all like to be a part.

We played in a lovely stadium but when the referee came into our dressing room he noticed that our shirts were without numbers. After a long argument when we realised that there was no way he was going to allow us to play, we agreed to swap into shirts provided by the home side.

The only problem with those shirts was that they were a very heavy woollen material and as the temperatures were still around 100°, they were not too popular with the players. We lost 3-0 and felt certain that those shirts were kept especially for the opposition. We haven't made that same mistake since, making sure that the shirts we take with us are always numbered.

Our final game in Ancona turned out to be a close second to the game at Elche. Ancona played in the Italian Third Division and the week before our game had drawn a friendly against the Scottish side Motherwell. When we arrived at the ground and saw the setup we knew that we were in for a tough game.

There were 4,000 people present and the game was played late at night under floodlights. All the side played magnificently but this was Roy Davies's finest hour. He stopped everything that Ancona threw at him and we deserved our 0-0 draw. It is these kinds of performances that make everything worthwhile. Ancona put on a spread for both teams that went on until late in the night. I hadn't told Mr. Wiess about this trip and thought we did quite well without him.

It was around this time that we decided Grasmere Rovers were to add a new dimension to the Sunday set up and introduce a side playing on Saturdays in the Manchester League. We were very pleased to get into a League of this status as it is undoubtedly the top amateur League in the area. The Sunday side had done well winning Cup and League matches and we felt that the only way we could improve ourselves was to move into Saturday football. This has since been proved the right decision.

How many times have we said that football is a funny game? The Ancona performance was quite magnificent. All the team had played out of their skins in alien surroundings against a semi-professional side from the Italian Third Division. That weekend we returned to Manchester and on the Monday evening we opened our League fixtures against Chadderton Reserves. Without any disrespect to Chadderton - who are a fine club with ambitions on a par to ours - it was a different situation than the one we had faced in Ancona.

Nine members of that 0-0 draw faced Chadderton and as we sat back waiting for the two points, it was a shock to the system when we were defeated 3-1. The style of football was so different but it proves that there isn't a team that can just go out and expect to win. Football is all about hard work, organisation and scoring goals where complacency doesn't play any part of the set up. We usually learn the hard way, although some people don't ever learn.

The following year we revisited the Costa Brava in Spain and based ourselves in Calella. Two more games were played against Lloret - and lost with the crowds in both games down to more manageable proportions. We then travelled up into the mountains and played against a team called Olot. They had a wonderful playing surface and quite a fair side too. We lost 4-1 to register another defeat, but it all goes down as good experience and all the time we are making friends.

The final game on this trip was against Calella and we marginally improved our playing record with a 4-1 win. To win any game of football usually brings a different and exciting atmosphere to the dressing room. Everyone is laughing and life appears to be worth living again.

After the Calella game we returned to our hotel and planned a party for the night. Everyone was enjoying themselves but one member of the team was sat quietly on his own in the corner of the room. The music and the joy of the evening was apparently going well over the top of his head as he was oblivious to what was going on around him.

I approached Wally Roberts to see if I could help to possibly solve some of his problems.

"What's wrong Wally", I asked.

Wally looked up at me and gave a sigh as he finally explained that he wasn't happy with the performance of the team against Calella. Wally was a good player who didn't break into professional football because he lacked pace. He played at Rossendale and several part time professional sides, but his obvious skills were hindered by this lack of pace and temperament.

He was, however, a deep thinker of the game and expected everything on the pitch to be perfect. We spent two hours talking about the usual problems in football whilst everyone was enjoying themselves. I didn't mind, it was good to have someone like Wally around who thought about the game so much. A pity he expected too much from players.

Several of the people who have travelled on our overseas tours have married girls who they have met whilst on tour. Keith Bateman met and married Jean Halton; Wally Roberts met and married Susan Gray who is the sister of one of our players, Ian Gray; Mike Cuerden met Jean Taylor and Ken Tidmas met a girl in Italy during one of our trips and they are now happily married. These tours appear to do more than just provide a game of football!

The trip in 1973 was back to Lido di Jesolo, this time of course a direct flight from Manchester to Venice that took just two hours. When I look back and remember my fear of flying, it is so hard to believe the change that has taken place in my attitude about travelling. All I want to do now is to get there. Then I was frightened of flying and enjoyed travelling the long way round just to see all the different places on the way.

Now it was a window seat and taking everything in that goes on during the flight. The old prop jet had been replaced by faster aircraft and I was really excited by this great way of travelling.

Prior to this trip a friend had put me in touch with a gentleman in Padua and in turn we managed to enter ourselves into a local tournament. I thought this sounded quite exciting as we had never entered a tournament before and to think that we would be in competition against foreign sides, as opposed to playing friendly teams, really appealed to my ambitious nature.

We travelled to Italy with several guest players who were older than the usual age of players we took on the tours. Billy Moores and Dawson Lane were two very experienced players from Manchester football along with Roy Davies. They would bring great experience to my team, I thought.

It was two days before the start of the tournament when we received details of the other teams taking part. Torino were in our group along with another Italian First Division side Lanerossi Vicenza. It was explained to us then that this was a Youth Tournament! Billy Moores, Dawson Lane and Roy Davies were in their thirties and we only had a small squad of players.

They had to play, otherwise we wouldn't have had a full team. We could pull out but that would have caused problems with the tournament organisers. We decided to go ahead. For Billy and Dawson, it wasn't too much of a problem to make them look young! It was Roy Davies who was the problem. For Roy had his black moustache and white hair!

However were we going to make Roy look under 21 when he had a black moustache and white hair? Well it was easy enough to shave off his moustache but Roy didn't take too kindly to our idea of covering his hair with black boot polish. Roy has had white hair from a very early age and of course it makes him look a lot older than he really is.

The ironic point that emerged from this trip was that for many years we had a young side playing against older players and just the year that we have an experienced side, we found ourselves by mistake in a youth competition!

We entered the Trofeo Pietro Galterossa that had as its previous winners Torino, Bologna and Partizan Belgrade. We opened the tournament against the local team Petraca and a large crowd watched us go down 2-0. It was good to play a club with the international standing of Torino and we did well to lose 1-0. More defeats on this tour, but I can never stress too much the great experience gained by the players.

Accompanying us on this trip - and many others - was Wilf Ashley: almost ready for retirement, he was still refereeing and dancing around like a two year old. Wilf never felt out of place with younger people as, in fact, he could always keep pace with their activities. He was a Commissionaire at the Manchester Stock Exchange and he was very involved with local amateur soccer. His father had run the old Corinthian Ladies team who had travelled all over the world.

Wilf really was a character. He used to be very keen on entering the "Spot the Ball" competitions and one day in the early seventies he won £4,500 with the Manchester Evening News. Now that kind of money was really worth something at that time. In fact, he went out and bought a new Ford Escort for £825.00. Wilf always had one motive in life - to enjoy himself - and to put £4,500 into his pocket was a licence for him to have a beano!

For ten months Wilf had a great time until he realised that he had spent every penny. To be fair to Wilf he took the whole Stock Exchange Staff to the Golden Garter Nightclub for a fantastic evening and when the Treasurer of the Manchester and District League had absconded with all the funds -some £1,200 - Wilf, along with Keith Bateman, came to the rescue with £600 each. Yes, Wilf had a kind heart.

He also had a knack of getting his picture on the front pages of the newspapers. He of course made the papers with his win on "Spot the Ball" then a few weeks later he was photographed greeting Miss United Kingdom to The Stock Exchange. He always looked smart in his uniform and top hat.

The third time he made the newspapers was the funniest of all. At the time I was working at the Stock Exchange and early one morning I was looking for Wilf. We found him outside the building which is in the heart of Manchester, perched on a high ledge looking absolutely petrified as he hung on clutching the side of the wall.

We dialled 999 and eventually a fire engine arrived to relieve Wilf of his misery. He had apparently been looking out of a window and had seen a pigeon stuck on the ledge, caught in a piece of string. Wilf, thinking that he would do his good deed for the day, decided to crawl out along the ledge and free the pigeon. Our hero had finally got to the pigeon and as he reached out to try and free it , he only succeeded in pulling the string tighter and strangling the poor thing! Wilf was that kind of person - always had good intentions but many of his actions ended just like Michael Crawford aka Frank Spencer!

7

Bulls and bears

All my working life I had been involved with The Stock Exchange and Stocks & Shares. I started on the market floor of the Manchester Exchange and what a great experience that was. It was enthralling just to watch the "dealers" in action. To look at the action resembled a mad house. People were rushing about, pointing, shouting, banging telephones down, many wearing top hats and other writing frantically.

Emerging from the chaos was millions of pounds as shares in companies were bought and sold as the investing public passed orders through to their stockbrokers. Somebody would telephone their broker and say they would like to buy 100 shares in ICI . The order would be passed on from the office to the dealer on the market floor and he would then try to buy the shares at the cheapest possible price. In those days on the Manchester exchange there were four jobbers. They are the people who act as wholesalers in shares.

The Jobber would quote two prices, say 702 to 706. That means that the shares could be bought for 706 and sold at 702. The Jobber is unaware of your intentions when he quotes a price. Another Jobber could be making the shares 701 to 705, so it would be cheaper to buy the shares from him. If you were a seller then the first Jobber was offering a better price.

It was all very exciting and very difficult to realise that so much money - in value - was being traded by just word of mouth.

The Stock Exchange motto is "my word is my bond" and it certainly has to be. Every firm of Stockbrokers are members of the Stock Exchange and have to abide by the very strict rules and regulations. You pay for the shares on account day which is usually every fortnight. If you have sold shares then payment would be received on that day.

My first job on the market was to mark the deals on a huge blackboard and excitedly watch the dealing on the floor. I spent exactly a year working on The Stock Exchange before I moved into the office of D Q Henriques who were a large firm of Manchester Stockbrokers. I slowly learned the "trade" of stockbroking amid an office background of scandal and corruption that would have made it a top seller as a weekly series on TV. Nothing would have to be altered for the running of the office to make avid viewing.

Take the most likeable cashier who unknown to everyone over a period of years managed to abscond over £7,000. Finally he was caught, admitted the crime and was sent to prison for one year. I went to see him in an open prison in Milnthorpe to find him really enjoying himself. In fact, it was just like Butlins Holiday Camp. Attractive gardens where prisoners could stroll pleasantly around, a games room, and our friend was in charge of the sports section! He was enjoying himself in prison and must have been disappointed when he did only nine months of his one-year sentence.

Our friend, who of course shall remain nameless, had worked for over 30 years at Henriques and was amazingly given the chance of having his job back at the firm. The Senior Partner decided that he would let the staff decide whether he was to be given another chance of working for the firm from which he had just stolen £7,000! Being such a friendly and likeable person the ballot in the office recorded a massive YES vote and the following week our friend returned to work.

How many firms would re-employ someone who had absconded with £7,000, most which was still hidden years later - probably in some Swiss bank account? Needless to say our friend wasn't put in charge of the cash again.

Every office has its scandal but this one had a very special one of its own. However, some of the people who worked there were great friends. Keith Young was a very special friend and there was Mr. Fish who shared my interests in cricket and music with Ronnie Burns and Peter Barlow.

Then there was Mike Fennell who was a partner in the firm. Mad Mike started as a junior at Henriques and whilst I was teaching him company dividends he used to beat me too many times at "hangman". Mike certainly was mad in his younger days. I remember him driving his Fiat car into a tree. Well, I suppose it's different! Then there was the time he was returning to the office at mid-day and decided that he would jump from car roof to car roof. As he made his way along the line of parked cars he failed to see that one had its roof rack open and jumped straight into the front seat! That was Mike, always good for a laugh. He's calmed down now, slightly, but he still has a passion for cars.

It was at Henriques where I earned my first bonus that took me on that initial trip to Majorca. My twelve years as a Stockbrokers' Clerk were hectic years as we had so many busy periods. Working overtime became a habit for many years. Sometimes, we would start at 9.00 in the morning and work straight through until midnight. All for overtime at 2s. 6d. an hour.

I became bored with life there eventually and felt I needed a change. When the Senior Partner announced that HE thought that the staff would prefer to work in new offices rather than have a bonus, I definitely decided that it was time to move out. (I was better out of the place.)

I went back to The Stock Exchange as Company Announcements Officer and spent four years on the Exchange where I started my career. My football career had given me great experience in organising and administration and I felt that it was time I got paid for doing that kind of job.

That's when I applied for the vacancy of Office Manager at Fernyhough & Co. and I was thrilled to get a position where I could utilise my appetite for administration. I had been at Fernyhough for two years when I was given one of the greatest honours of my life.

The then Senior Partner Derek Smith told me that they would like me to apply for membership of The Stock Exchange. To become a Member now would mean having to pass a lot of special examinations, but I managed to qualify with my experience in the business. Members of the Stock Exchange are all partners or associate partners of their firms and I was to be a member of that exclusive club.

I was proposed and seconded by two Members outside my firm and attended an interview in front of the local Stock Exchange committee. My firm's application for me to become a Member was accepted and my big day soon arrived.

The Stock Exchange where I had stood and stared at the frantic activity years before was that day to become my stage. At 2.30 p.m. the Chairman banged his hammer and if by magic, the shouting ceased, everyone sat down and a rare scene of peace and tranquillity covered the market floor as I stood shaking, waiting for my big moment.

The Chairman began his speech and briefly told the silent audience about my career in stockbroking. Then came that very special proud moment when I walked across the floor of The Stock Exchange to loud applause. I was a Stockbroker, and everyone came across to shake my hand. Being a rather quiet and unassuming kind of person, I felt embarrassed, but it couldn't hide my pride. It was one of those very special moments that will remain in the memory for the rest of my life.

One disappointment that was caused through working late hours at Henriques was having to give up taking piano lessons. At a very early age I started to play the piano and although I didn't take it as seriously as I should have done, I managed to pass six exams. I failed the seventh exam when there was just no time to practice with working so many late hours - a pity because the eighth exam was the final one and it would have been nice to achieve some letters after my name. I stopped after that failure but it hasn't dampened my enthusiasm for good music.

Manchester Stock Exchange today with plans in hand to turn it into a luxury hotel.

8

The court line crash

It was now 1974 and in the previous eleven tours we had covered most of Europe. The urge was to go further afield without the cost escalating too much and being well out of reach of most people's budget. I saw the possibilities of going to Southern Spain and maybe nipping over to North Africa. This appealed to me so I booked a fortnight in Torremolinos with a straightforward package tour from Manchester. Notice the comment there "straightforward." Later events were to make it anything but straightforward.

After arranging for our opening games to be in Spain, I made contact with the football authorities in Morocco and was thrilled to get a reply that they had organised a tournament especially for us in Tangiers. There would be four teams taking part: ourselves, Tangiers, Tetuan from Morocco and Algeciras from Spain. The Tangier club offered to pay our fares from Malaga and return.

I was very excited by this as it would be our first game outside Europe in a new continent, Africa. The final coup was organising a game in a place called Melilla which is in Spanish Morocco and was done through one of our players, Rafael Cabrera. Rafael was born in Melilla and moved with his parents to England when he was 14. He was coming on the trip with us so this was a good opportunity for him to see his place of birth again.

Before our departure I was looking forward to the trip more than any other. The football looked really exciting and to actually think we were going to Tangier gave me the same kind of thrill as when I experienced my first trip abroad.

It was the Thursday evening before the Sunday we were to leave for Spain. Our first game was to be in a place called Ronda on the Saturday evening. I had been to a Committee meeting of the Manchester & District League and on arriving home about 10.30 I was met by my mother who tearfully announced that the holiday was off. I half smiled. How could it be off, yet the tears in her eyes were obviously there for a purpose.

We should have been travelling by Court Line and it had just been announced on the news that the airline had gone into liquidation and no more flights would be taking off. I was shattered! At that time in the evening there wasn't a lot I could do, but I felt as though I had to do something. The phone rang. It was Ian Halfpenny and we decided that we would go down immediately to Manchester Airport and attempt to rectify the situation.

What we expected to do at 11.00 in the evening I will never know but we felt that we had to be there on the scene. The airport was almost deserted and nobody could obviously do a thing. I spent a sleepless night. The tournament in Africa seemed a continent away.

The following day, Friday, was spent on the telephone. Our travel company was trying to make alternative arrangements for us to get away. We were offered holidays in Majorca, Ibiza and various parts of Spain, but I insisted that all we wanted was a flight to Malaga. There were 30 in our party and of course they were anxious to find out what was happening. The phone didn't stop ringing but as Saturday morning approached we were no nearer finding a way to Spain.

We should have been leaving that morning but it was even more exasperating to be sat at home when we should have been on our way. Then around 4.00 p.m. on the Saturday afternoon, a telephone call came from the travel company to tell me that they had got us on a flight from Manchester to Malaga leaving at 8.00am on the Sunday – magic! Everyone was overjoyed. We would be in Spain just in time for our first game in Ronda during the evening.

At 7.00am we reported at Manchester's Ringway airport for our Dan Air flight to Malaga. Never was I so pleased to see a Dan Air Comet. They were the first jet aircraft and previous bumpy trips across Europe signalled that they were coming to the end of an illustrious career. This particular day, that aircraft was a saviour.

Everyone in the party was there early, except one person. Tim Ingham was coming on his first trip and this day was to mark the beginning of experiencing an amazing character. Tim is invariably always late. He is an executive of a leading advertising firm and most of Tim's life was spent at work. His father is the Managing Director so Tim probably feels some allegiance to putting in the hours, but that doesn't excuse him for turning up late everywhere he goes.

He finally roared into the airport terminal at 7.45 a.m. just as everyone was boarding the aircraft. I was to share a room with Tim - I'd show him how to be punctual!

We arrived in Malaga and were taken to our hotel. That was the next shock. What a dump! In all our travels abroad, this was the worst hotel I'd ever seen. I immediately asked our courier to find us alternative accommodation as soon as possible. No way would we stay there, even for one night. No sooner had we arrived than a coach turned up to take us to the game. I thought we needed a rest before we departed as it was only two inches on the map to Ronda. It was 3.00pm and I thought we had plenty of time so the players were told to rest in their rooms - along with the ants!

Foolishly, I refused to listen to the coach driver who told me it was a three-hour journey to Ronda. At 4.00pm we left, apparently in plenty of time for the 7.00pm kick off. We left with the courier promising to find us alternative accommodation.

Those two inches on the map turned out exactly as the coach driver had said - a three-hour journey. The trip to Ronda was up tortuous mountain roads and I realised that I should have done more homework on the journey.

We finally arrived in a beautiful town right in the middle of the Sierra Nevada. Ronda has the oldest bull ring in the world. As we passed the colourful entrance the thought did pass my mind that we may be going to our own slaughter.

As we approached the ground with just ten minutes to kick off we saw posters with our photographs staring down at us and the pretty town seemed alive as everyone appeared to be heading in the direction of the football ground. We were late arriving but at least we had got there, better late than never. I remember sitting next to Tim on the coach and he seemed petrified at the number of people going to the game. For someone only used to playing on a park ground it must have been quite an experience.

This was a big game for the local side and they had decided to import some players just for the match. They proved too good for us and we went down 4-0. The full day's travelling had taken its toll and we made the journey back to Torremolinos in the early hours of the morning, hoping that our courier had had more success. We were not to be disappointed. On our return he had left a note to say that we were to be moved the following day into apartments and these turned out to be more than acceptable.

This particular trip was the first that Fred Eyre had joined and it was the start of a long association with someone who has had very varied experience in travel and football. Fred is a very proud person and although he didn't make it as a professional footballer, he is a true professional in everything he does.

His preparation for every game was always to perfection. When you hear of some top footballers who have had many misdemeanours in life it is a pity that someone like Fred, who dreamt of leading Manchester City out at Wembley and did all the correct things in life, just didn't get the breaks that his dedication deserved. He went on the slippery slope down the various Leagues and here he was with Grasmere on the first of many tours around the World.

Fred built a very successful stationery business through hard graft and ambition. His books - "Kicked into Touch" and "Another Breath of Fred Eyre" have become best sellers and have inspired me to put pen to paper in a similar vein. His books are famous for little anecdotes from his vast experience in the game of football.

One anecdote not mentioned in either of his books is the one about the fullback who was told before a game by his manager

"You've got too much skill to play at fullback, so I'm making you sub!"

As Fred's playing days finished he joined a local Manchester radio station and began to broadcast on local games. This part of the game too has a special art. I was with him one evening in the Press Box at Bury as they were playing my favourite team Stockport County. How many times have we heard the comment "Football's a funny game?"

Stockport were leading Bury 2-1 and as time ran out, looking comfortable winners. With just five minutes to go, Fred put the finishing touches to his end of match report, explaining how Stockport deserved their win, and as the local Bury crowd dispersed making angry comments that Bury wouldn't score if they played all night, suddenly the whole game changed.

Bury scored twice in the final three minutes to snatch a dramatic 3-2 win. All Fred's comments went flying through the air as he had to re-write his report at top speed in time to go on the air. Football is a funny game.

The highlight of the trip approached as we left Malaga by boat for the African continent and Tangier. Again, there was a tingle in the tummy as we sailed past Gibraltar and approached a new world. Tangier was more than an experience, in fact it was just like another world. The advice was not to walk around on your own and it was not difficult to see why.

So many shady people lurked in dark corners and as we walked about we must have stood out like sore thumbs. I have always fancied going into a casino and having a go at roulette. My first experience was in Romania when Wilf Ashley and I hit a winning streak. l had to have another go so I took Fred and Dave Brooks along and we joined the betting fraternity in a Tangiers casino.

I don't think Fred and Dave were too impressed and they soon left the table. I was so engrossed in the spinning wheel and dice that I didn't realise that both of them had disappeared! Hours later I left the table a little richer and realised that I had to make my way back to the hotel on my own. It was the early hours of the morning and I have never run so fast in all my life. The mile back to the Hotel didn't seem all that far as I sped through side streets passing all kinds of strange people. Was I glad to get back to our hotel. Tangier by day is bad enough but to be out alone at night ......

Playing football in a foreign country is always a new experience but playing football in Tangier was extra exciting with a touch of colour also added. Our first game was against Moroccan Second Division Champions Tetuan. In an effort to get the local people onto our side we decided to throw flowers into the crowds. The biggest problem was to get them over the high barbed wire fence that separated the ferocious crowd from the playing area. It didn't help much - we lost 6-0! The standard of football amazed me. We are only amateurs, but I totally misread the situation. Who would have thought that Moroccan football at Second Division level would be able to match a team from England? This was my first lesson that these so called unknown soccer countries are better than we think and are rapidly catching up with the established footballing nations.

When Tetuan scored their first goal I thought World War Three had broken out. Guns were fired into the air and smoke billowed over the stadium. I was horrified until from the middle of the crowd behind one goal, a band suddenly started to play. All this happened six times. There was hardly a dull moment. I wonder what happens to the band when it's a 0-0 draw?

We returned to the solitude of our smelly dressing room and made a great friend in the local attendant Mustapha. We asked him where the showers were and he pointed to a dingy room. When a player stepped into the room Mustapha would throw a bucket of water over him and shout in his best English "Next plees!"

The following day we were taken to meet the Governor of Tangier for an official reception at his palace. This was a wonderful and exotic experience meeting the local dignitaries and drinking mint tea. In the afternoon we visited the Kasbah and must have been stopped nearly a hundred times to buy every bit of rubbish imaginable.

I had really looked forward to visiting Tangier and I enjoyed the experience but water rationing in the hotel meant few washes and no bath. We still had to play the game against Algeciras for the third place play off but I longed to get back to civilised Spain.

We lost 2-0 against Algeciras in a better performance and enjoyed watching the Final between the two Moroccan sides. Tangier won 1-0 and the noise and excitement was another new experience.

It is no fun being in a hot country when there isn't any water in the taps. It was good to be back in Spain.

The final game on our tour provided us with the most excitement yet. Part of Northern Morocco is owned by Spain and Rafael Cabrera had worked hard to get us a game against his home town team, Melilla. They had agreed to fly the football side of our party from Malaga to Melilla in two small eight-seater Piper aircraft.

Considering my earlier fear of flying it was another remarkable case of how my whole attitude to flying had changed. We arrived at Malaga airport and as we walked across the tarmac to our small aircraft it was a little frightening to see how small the planes were. A Boeing 737 stood in the background and this smaller jet aircraft simply dwarfed our little Piper plane.

The journey took just under one hour and I sat behind the pilot. I would have enjoyed a ten-hour journey in this position being intrigued with everything that went on. It was exciting to see the runway in front of us and on touching down we all clapped the pilot on his brilliant landing. It was equally exciting watching the second aircraft appear over the distant hills with our remaining eight people.

Melilla was a pretty little town with spotless white houses, but I could see why Rafael and his family had settled down in England. There wasn't a lot to do; in fact, the place appeared to be a ghost town.

That couldn't be said for the football team or the hospitality of the Melilla club. They had a large ground and the local side played in the Spanish Third Division. Imagine every away game having to cross the Mediterranean by air or by sea. The same of course applies to teams on the islands of Majorca and Ibiza. Teams back home don't know they are born!

This final game of our tour turned out to be a disaster on the field as a very good side gave our tired team a right run-a-round and we lost 9-0. The irony of this game was a big scoreboard behind one goal. When it was 8-0 the scoreboard attendant stood there with the number nine in his hands. I was wishing he had dropped it on his foot! Good job it wasn't double figures, there wasn't any room on the board for that.

It was disappointing to suffer another defeat especially a heavy one. A lot of work goes into organising these matches but it really is so difficult playing football in a hot country whilst on holiday. Top professional sides playing in European competitions make sure that their players stay out of the sun and go to bed early. How can players who pay a lot of money to have a holiday be expected to keep those rules? To be fair to the players, most of them are dedicated but in many instances we are meeting sides who are several classes above our standard.

Again, it is always good to give players the experience of playing football abroad. I was pleased to see Norman Higginson and his wife Julie on this trip. Norman played many years for Grasmere and he spent a lot of spare time with his own pop group. He later had the honour of appearing at the London Palladium having won a local competition.

Another tour was over. From those early days when it was the thrill of a lifetime just to see the Northern coast of France, we had covered the length and breadth of Europe and had now actually been to Africa.

One interesting aspect of all these trips was the variation and different interpretation of referees. There's no doubt about it that referees can turn matches and many times abroad the referee is totally biased towards the home team.

I was interested in refereeing from an early part of my football life and in the late 1960's I decided to take up refereeing on a Saturday. I started in local leagues and began to enjoy the different concept from being involved with a team. When Grasmere joined The Manchester League in 1970 my refereeing took a back seat. A pity really as I felt that I was just beginning to make headway into a higher standard. I would have dearly liked to have reached the top.

One person who did was Neil Midgley. Neil refereed Grasmere Rovers several times in the Manchester League before he graduated through the Leagues and was one of the best referees in the country, if not the world. He would spend most nights during the week attending meetings and he became a successful after dinner speaker. Sadly, Neil died some years ago. He was a charming man who fully deserved his success.

There was one local Manchester referee Tommy Fairhurst who went on refereeing until he was 82, only four years before he passed away. He used to travel by bus all over the area and would do up to four games a week. All kinds of wonderful people make up this beautiful game of football.

The world of football is also full of marvellous stories about soccer. Most of them seem to come from abroad. Here is a selection.

In Peru, women are allowed to referee men's soccer matches and they have decided that complimentary remarks made to them during matches will be met with a red card. Apparently Peruvian players like to sweeten up their protests to the lady referees by adding a few polite words of flattery, such as "that was never a corner, my little dove" or "surely he was offside, my most cherished lovebird." As they say, flattery will get you nowhere except the dressing room!

In Argentina the referee in a local game was taking some "real" stick from the crowd so he handed his whistle to a wildly gesticulating fan saying "here, you have a go." The man took over but after awarding two penalties without any possible justification, he was bungled from the ground by the players and the game was abandoned.

A supporter in Australia was returning home in a bad mood after his team had been beaten. He aimed a vicious kick at an empty beer can and it landed on the chin of an attractive blonde. The supporter saw the girl home as blood oozed from her chin. The latest news is that they now plan to be married.

If you decide to play football in the village of Tengen-Wiechs, you will need a passport. The touchline on one side of the field is identical to the border of Germany and Switzerland. To take a corner kick or throw in means leaving the country! Fortunately, the home side are all members of German customs so they are lenient on political issues.

We hear much of large transfer fees - how's this for a change. A Norwegian Division Four side sold a player to Stavanger FC. The transfer fee was a pound of cheese, four pints of milk, four eggs, one small loaf and a pound of coffee. He must have been a bread and butter player!!

The £100,000 transfer fee that brought Kazio Deyna from Legia Warsaw to Manchester City was made up of £70,000 in cash with the balance in medical gear of which they are short in Poland.

St. Etienne, the famous French club, reckon they have cut the number of players suffering from colds and flu by 25%. Their method was to install ten hair dryers in the dressing room so the players don't go home from training with wet hair.

The team coach used by AC Milan must take some beating. It has showers, massage tables and even beds to make the journey to and from games just that little bit easier.

Five players were sent off in a recent match in Rosario, Argentina. The teams were made up of league referees!

A chap called Ponciano Rodrigez has been hitting the headlines in Peru. He does 90 minutes of exercises before playing for his local Sunday team. By the way, he is 80 years old.

In Peru there is a team called Los Terribles who in a recent League game fully lived up to their name - they were all sent off. With their side leading 1-0 all eleven players sat down on their goal line in protest at the referee's decision to award a penalty against them. After first giving all the players a yellow card, they still refused to move - so they all got the red card.

Paolo Ammoniacci of Palermo set a record in an Italian League game. He came on as substitute but was sent off by the referee after only eleven seconds.

Travelling to games can be hazardous in some countries, especially for referees. Recently in Brazil referee Nacor Arouche had to hire a taxi to get to his game in Boa Viste. However, the cab broke down late at night in thick jungle and an Indian tribe came to investigate. The ref was made to sit in pouring rain as the tribe pulled his hair and did a war dance round him. Another car came along and frightened them off but surely this never happened to Michael Oliver.

Then there is a funny story of the Brazilian player who was standing to attention for the National Anthem, only to suddenly dash back into the dressing room. He had to forget about national loyalty when an army of ants suddenly marched under his shorts!!

There are some great little stories from the world of football and long may they continue.

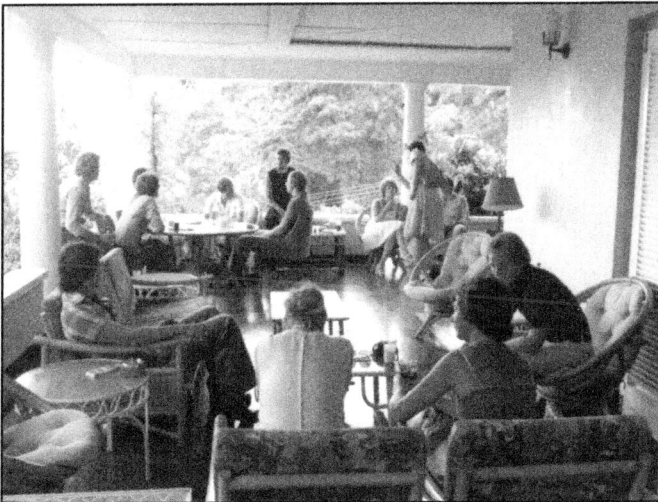

Relaxing as guests of the British Embassy in Trinidad in 1978

9

What Jamaica that?

The journey into Africa had broadened our horizons. We had inched further away from the British Isles and the appetite for adventure and travelling the world gathered momentum. I wondered if it was possible to travel even further. Very quickly jet travel was making it possible to go almost anywhere in the world.

Of course, there is never any limit on where we can go, but the most important point is whether people can afford it. I browsed through brochures and couldn't help but return to the pages that featured the Caribbean. Now that really did sound somewhere "magic". The prices in the brochures looked expensive so I went about finding ways of getting there cheaper.

The more I thought of the Caribbean, the more I was determined to get there. I made frequent visits to the British Airways office in Manchester and found Bob Watson most helpful. We decided that to do a separate flight and accommodation would work out cheaper. That was it; I decided to go ahead and as in all my early preparation of a tour, nobody was told in advance.

I liked the look of Jamaica and found their Tourist Office in London very helpful with regards to organising accommodation in several beautiful villas.

I attended a Grasmere Committee Meeting and put my proposition forward. "It was a great idea," they said, "but it won't work". Those comments went over my head. I would prove them wrong. I circulated all members of the club plus friends who had travelled with us before. I quoted the cost as around £175.00 each which included air travel from Manchester to London, London to Kingston Jamaica and accommodation in a luxury villa. Even in 1975 that was tremendous value.

The response was electric. Within no time the holiday was fully booked with 30 people wanting to take part in this holiday of a lifetime. Travel from London to Kingston was in a Jumbo which in those days added to the excitement. Then a coach journey to that magical sounding place, Montego Bay.

I could think of nothing else but Jamaica. I had written to their Football Association and received a reply that a game would be arranged in Kingston against their National side. The excitement was slowly building and I began to feel more ambitious. I was constantly looking at maps of the area and began to wonder whether we could perhaps encompass other countries around Jamaica.

To travel so far and just visit one country seemed rather inadequate so I wrote to the Football Association of Haiti which was just across the water from Jamaica - well around 400 miles! A few weeks later I received a reply and was delighted that they were to arrange a game for us against their top league side Violette in Port-au-Prince.

My imagination and ambition were now running riot. The map of the Caribbean took some more hammer as I measured distances and looked again and again at a place called Cuba. Surely, they would be pleased to entertain us! Another letter was sent and I awaited a reply from the country Fidel Castro had invaded and gained many enemies throughout the world.

The reply came from the Cuban Embassy in London and I couldn't believe my luck when they said that the Cuban Football Federation would be honoured to play a game against us. For both the Haiti and Cuban game I had asked for them to pay our flight from Jamaica and return. They had agreed to these conditions plus two nights' accommodation.

I have never looked forward to a holiday as much as I did this one. A holiday in the Caribbean, accommodation in a luxury

Villa with trips to Haiti and Cuba thrown in for good measure. My mother warned me not to look forward to the holiday too much as it may prove to be an anti-climax. I took her point but there was so much to absorb in this one and it took a lot to put it to the back of my mind.

The day of departure slowly, very slowly at first, arrived. There had been problems in obtaining Visas from the Cuban Embassy. The forms that required filling in wanted everyone's life history but they were forwarded straight to Kingston awaiting our arrival in Jamaica.

Saturday 14th June, 1975 and we met at Manchester's Ringway Airport for the short flight to London. On arrival at Heathrow we were taken for morning coffee and refreshments. VIP treatment already. The excitement was now really building up as we made our way to Terminal Three for our British Airways Jumbo jet to Kingston, Jamaica.

We weren't disappointed. The spacious Jumbo's were so much better than previous smaller aircraft. Just as I had been sceptical on my first ever flight, I was now eager not to miss a single event of what was now going on. We had a ten-hour flight with a stop in Bermuda. The plane was only half full so it was very comfortable. The meals were superb and then we settled down to watch a film. This is the life.

The flight of course was the longest I had flown so far and after around six hours we started to make our descent into Bermuda. I couldn't wait to get a glimpse of that magic sounding place. As we approached the ground, the coral reefs and white sand beaches looked fantastic. Then as we landed I realised it was raining. Fancy raining in Bermuda!

There was no such problem on arriving in Kingston. As we had circled over the capital the National Stadium where we were to play our game stood out and looked very imposing.

On arrival in the airport lounge we were greeted by a Jamaican rum punch and a sign which said "We apologise for the inconvenience whilst we modernise our airport, soon everything will be beautiful just for you". I will always remember those words; they made me feel welcome, although the rum punch possibly helped!

We had a coach to take us the 120 miles from Kingston to Montego Bay. One thing I didn't realise was that the journey was over mountains and rough roads. A journey I thought would take around three hours took six. We finally arrived at our Villas at 1.00 a.m. that being six hours behind English time so we were obviously very tired.

Each of our three Villas had a cook, a maid and a gardener and even at that time in the morning they were waiting for us to arrive. There were ten people in each Villa, and each Villa had five bedrooms with adjoining toilets, a lounge, dining room, kitchen and swimming pool surrounded by a patio.

Despite the long journey myself and room mate Brian Kellock were up early in the morning and the scene didn't disappoint us. The hot sun helped to make everywhere look absolutely magnificent. I couldn't believe that we were really there. The sea in the distance shimmered - we must make an early visit to sample the Caribbean.

The first few days were paradise. Jamaica is a very scenic island, with the Blue Mountains in the centre of the island separating Montego Bay in the north and the capital Kingston in the South.

Two visits we made stand out as spectacular and will always be remembered by all who took part. Firstly, -we went to the Jamaica Swamp Safari which houses crocodiles and alligators. The James Bond film "Live and Let Die", has a scene taken from the swamp and it was exciting walking down a narrow path with the gamekeeper banging his stick on the crocodile's heads as they crawled out of the water and snapped at us as we walked by.

I had my cine camera recording every moment and was so engrossed in taking a film of one crocodile crawling along the path towards me that I didn't realise the imminent danger I was in. The gamekeeper who had assisted Roger Moore in the film, snapped at me and I hurriedly made a panicky retreat. A notice in the water said "No swimming allowed." Nobody I'm sure would ever dream of it.

The other place that produced a memorable experience was the waterfall at Ocho Rios. This was a waterfall which had steps for people to scramble up through the swirling water. The start of the accent was on the beautiful beach and although the climb was precarious the roaring water helped to cool down those tired limbs.

Both these places produced an experience of seeing and doing something that was so different to anything else we had ever done.

Before we had arrived in Jamaica we had heard of the terrible violence that existed in that country. Crime in Kingston was at a higher level than in New York. Despite the beauty of the country there was a little fear every time we walked out, especially at night. One morning we heard that someone had been shot dead the previous night in Montego Bay. That sent a cold shiver down the spine as one wondered what was waiting around every corner.

Poverty in Jamaica is very high, particularly in Kingston. People live in tin huts and never see any of the luxuries that we take for granted. This was the first time that I had seen real poverty and it made me wonder why we in England moan so much about our living standards.

The only problem I had in our Villa was the lack of a telephone. This is such a vital commodity when we go on these football tours. Teams want to contact me to make those final arrangements and I wish to contact them too as most foreign soccer officials are very lax with their correspondence.

I had to walk around 500 yards to another Villa where the occupants — American of course — kindly allowed me to make contact with the outside world. There was so much organising to do on this trip with flights to other countries to arrange. It wasn't helped by the Jamaican Football Association switching the date of our game to a different day.

Our first game on the tour was in Montego Bay against a local team called Perfectos. They weren't very perfect with the arrangements as we arrived at the ground to find a stubborn cow grazing on the pitch. It is difficult enough playing football in a foreign country against eleven players, a biased referee, and a blazing hot sun, without having to dribble the ball past a cow as well!

We won the match 1-0 and tried to give everyone in the squad a game to give them experience before the big ones ahead. Roy Jones scored the goal.

We were now ready for our first big game on the island of Haiti. The few days spent on this voodoo island opened my eyes more than any time in my life. Haiti is classed as the seventh poorest country in the world. Its ruler Papa Doc was well known for the terror his dictatorial power had ruled over the years. More recently his son "Baby Doc" had taken over and when he arranged his wedding a few years ago he spent more than two million pounds on a very sumptuous affair. He invited lots of famous people, but most of them failed to turn up. They stayed away in protest about his family's policies over many years and the amount of money spent on the wedding, when there were millions of people in Haiti living in poverty.

We were booked onto an American Eastern Airlines flight from Montego Bay to Port-au-Prince. Our tickets had been organised by the Violette Club in Haiti and when we arrived at the airport there was chaos as airline officials searched for our tickets and appeared to make out that we were not booked onto the flight.

After a while everything was sorted out and we eventually made our way onto the aircraft. The plane was by now 20 minutes late leaving and we boarded with the voice of the pilot coming through the inter-com.

"We apologise for the late take-off ladies and gentlemen but we have had a little problem with an English soccer team coming on board".

We left Montego Bay behind and just over an hour later made our landing at Port-au-Prince airport in Haiti. As we stepped off the plane we were met by officials of the Violette club and I met for the first time Antionne Tassy who was Lord High Everybody of the Club.

Mr. Tassy was a member of FIFA and had managed the Haiti World Cup team the previous year in Germany. He was a small man wearing glasses, but he held the power of football in Haiti and was one of the few wealthy men in the country.

We were rushed through customs and I couldn't help thinking

how small and sparse the airport was seeing that we were in the Capital City. Outside waiting for us was a convoy of cars that was to ferry our party to the Hotel. I sat in the front car and it was then that I blinked in surprise as I saw that we were to be led by a police escort. As we drove from the airport we had the police siren screeching and a tape in our car announcing to people in French that Manchester AFC had arrived and not to forget to go and see the big game tomorrow night. This was exciting but also a little frightening as we realised how big the game was going to be.

People stood and stared at us as we roared past and then we saw why Haiti is so poor. The buildings were old, public transport meant sitting in the back of a van. There were people everywhere, some sitting on the soiled pavements others leaning on walls, the rest just standing around in groups. We were 6,000 miles from home and the scene made us feel every mile of it away.

We arrived at our hotel called "The Coconut Villa" and were pleasantly surprised at the standards. It had a good swimming pool and on the far side was a wall which was scaled by hawkers selling various bits of rubbish at astronomical prices. They enjoyed bartering with our party and many people got all kinds of bargains to take home from Haiti.

The next morning, we decided to visit the stadium for a loosener and were amazed on arrival to find that nearly 3,000 people had turned up just to watch us training.

The game was to kick off at 8.30 in the evening and on arrival at the ground one hour before, the atmosphere was already feeling electric. This was the very same ground that two years earlier in a World Cup qualifying game between Haiti and Cuba a spectator had produced a gun and shot somebody, and Haiti had won too. In that same game Haiti had qualified for the finals and there had been dramatic scenes as the locals celebrated victory.

Two years later in 1976, again against Cuba, six people had been killed after police had opened fire when a spectator had let off a firecracker. It seemed a dangerous place to be in, but nothing was going to stop us playing now.

Our massive dressing room had a police guard both inside and outside and for the first time we learnt that the game was to be televised live throughout Haiti. It was getting more terrifying by the minute. Dave Brooks was being interviewed by the radio station as he was the only person in our party who could speak French.

Our captain Wally Roberts led our team out between a police escort and the whole place looked weird. A sea of black faces surrounded the playing area but I sensed that the occasion was friendly and failed to detect any hostility. Only two English clubs had visited Haiti previously, Chelsea led by Tommy Docherty and Wolves. We were the third team being fed to the lions.

The captain of Violette was making his first appearance since being "sent home" by Haiti from Germany for taking drugs before a World Cup game. To strengthen their side Violette played two Argentinian forwards, as if they needed to strengthen their team! Here we were, thousands of miles from home in a strange hot country, playing their top League club that already boasted several internationals, and all they wanted to do was strengthen their side.

From our point of view, we had a good team, but in those kinds of conditions it was just like starting the game two goals down. The crowd was reported as 11,000, although it seemed many more as they made a lot of noise every time our goal area was attacked.

Our goalkeeper Keith Jones must have had nightmares for weeks after as the Haiti forwards bore down upon him.

We lost the game 3-0 but put up a very creditable performance under the conditions. Not many foreign sides come to Port-au-Prince and win. After the game the players were physically exhausted, but they had put on a tremendous performance against all the odds.

That evening I was taken out for a meal by Mr. Tassy along with Keith and Jean Bateman. We were the only people in the restaurant. Perhaps we were the only people in Port-au-Prince who could afford to dine out. We had an excellent meal and Mr. Tassy told us many interesting stories of his football life.

Mr. Tassy had been on the organising committee that planned the

World Cup in England during 1966. He had lunch at 10 Downing Street with Prime Minister Harold Wilson prior to the Final, but the one person he really enjoyed meeting was Tommy Docherty.

"Give my regards to Mr. Tommy", he kept telling me during the meal. The Doc was then at Old Trafford as manager of Manchester United and when I returned to England I passed on the message to the Doc.

"A great little character", the Doc replied when I rang him, "but what a terrible place", he continued.

The following day we went on a shopping expedition into the centre of Port-au-Prince. What an experience that was. There were people everywhere and most of our party were too frightened to go off alone.

We were taken to a large square where stood possibly the only imposing building in Haiti. It just had to be Papa Doc's Palace. I stood and stared at the place where Jean Claude Duvalier, the 20 stone playboy, lived. The tanks and anti-aircraft guns in the gardens gave the gleaming white building a forbidding look.

He had been left a very difficult task by his father to manage a country where the average annual wage was £65 and the life expectancy around 40. The people are bankrupt and so is the country. Foreign aid is very sparse as people still remember Papa Doc and no country wishes to be observed propping up a tyranny.

The United States has lately been showing an interest in this Caribbean island. They can produce cheap labour. Maybe they will help it to get rid of the past history of torture and poverty.

We left Haiti very quickly; we had to as we were late leaving for the airport. I left a pair of brown shoes under the bed in the hotel. Perhaps some Haitian was glad of them, but as we winged out of Port-au-Prince back to Montego Bay I had to rub my eyes and pinch myself to confirm that it had all really happened.

Coconut Villa Hotel

VILLAGE LAMOTHE — DELMAS — PHONE : 2-3600

C/o OSO BLANCO

PHONE : 2-3339

PORT-AU-PRINCE, HAITI

1967 Lloret trip. Taken before our game in Alcoy, Spain. Picture includes: Roy Reed, second left at back, one of our best centre halves and front row third from right Paul Fitzgerald who went on to play for Hyde United. Some may recognise Dave Booth and Billy Headland front right. Also John Rogan third left at the front who was unlucky to be sent off agianst Elche in our famous 1-0 victory over Di Stefano's youth team.

Back home showing off our souvenirs after our tour of Jamaica, Haiti and Cuba. Fred Eyre (front left) Paul Fitzgerald (front right) and also there: Dave Brooks, Roy Davies, Eddie Cuncarr, Roy Jones, Wally Roberts, Bernard Pevoy and Stuart Drummond. Kneeling at the front is Keith Jones and Brian Kellock.

10

Our men in Havana

The following few days in our Villas at Montego Bay were like paradise. The hot sun, gorgeous white sandy beaches, wavering palm trees, colourful flowering shrubs everywhere and a happy bunch of people that were enjoying a wonderful new experience.

Our next game was in Kingston against the Jamaican National team, but we didn't relish that awful journey again over the Blue Mountains by a rickety coach. However, it had to be and after five hours bumping over all kinds of roads we finally made it to the National Stadium.

Football in Jamaica is not on the same level as in Haiti or even Cuba but any game against a National side in a hot foreign country was going to be a difficult one. The stadium was impressive. Some years ago, it had held the Commonwealth Games and George Foreman had knocked out Joe Frazier for the Heavyweight Championship of the World. There were around 3,000 people present which showed the lack of enthusiasm in the country for its National team. The game was badly advertised and just proved how inexperienced the officials were in organising a football game. The match was sponsored by Guinness and the officials must have thought that there was nothing else to do. I don't know whether it was good for them or not!

The game turned out to be a real battle. The referee was called Chaplin and he was on the FIFA list, but what a right Charlie he was. He sent three players off, two of ours and had real difficulties in controlling the game. We battled well and although we went close with shots from Brian Kellock and Ian Halfpenny we managed to hold out for a 0-0 draw.

I will always remember before the game I was paid an unusual compliment by one of the players during my team talk. I was in the middle of getting everybody wound up for the game when I suddenly heard a snore. I turned around to see Eddie Cuncarr lying on the table fast asleep! I'll have to make them more interesting next time. We nicknamed Eddie, Rip Van Winkle after that.

The holiday was nearing its end but we still had one big game to play. We had done so much already since leaving England, but on the day, we were to depart for Cuba I received a big shock. Some of our party weren't too keen on another coach journey to Kingston to meet up with our flight to Havana. I wasn't too keen myself but so much work had been put into this part of the tour.

A meeting was held and it was Fred Eyre who came up with a great idea. Our flight tickets home we found out could be used from Montego Bay to Kingston. By flying we cut out that terrible coach journey. That did it, but the flight to Kingston was leaving in one hour's time. We rushed around to get ourselves ready and with the help of two hired cars driven by myself and Keith Bateman and some taxis we dashed to the nearby airport and breathlessly checked onto the flight.

The other big difficulty was that we were not returning to Montego Bay as when we came back from Cuba we were connecting with our flight home from Kingston. This meant packing all our baggage and leaving some in the luggage office in Kingston.

As we flew out of Montego Bay I took a last longing look at the place that had fulfilled a dream and provided memories that will last forever. A pity we had to leave in such a hurry.

Our flight to Havana was an hour late in arriving from Barbados. The Cuban Airlines officials in Kingston airport were anything but lax. They were fussy and officious as they poured over our visas and passports. At one stage it appeared as if they were going to prevent us from boarding the plane.

Finally, we boarded and around two hours late we headed into the darkness towards Fidel Castro's Cuba. Our party of 30 helped to fill the aircraft but the small propeller plane had a strange atmosphere as we were stared at continuously by the Cuban passengers as though we were aliens. Thinking about it, I suppose we were.

It was around 9.00 p.m. when we touched down in Havana. We disembarked and hardly had I stepped foot on Cuban soil than three swarthy gentlemen approached us. They turned out to be from Intersport, the Cuban Sporting organisation who were in charge of organising the game.

Myself, Keith Bateman and Dave Jones, as officials of the club, were taken on one side and we approached a door which suddenly opened. I glanced inside to see about a dozen people sat around a table. When they saw me, everybody suddenly stood to attention? I felt very embarrassed as we were led to the head of the table. An attractive lady appeared and introduced herself as our interpreter. She explained that this was a press conference.

The importance of the whole occasion suddenly dawned on me. I thought of the indecision as to whether we should come to Cuba and then blinked as the cameramen took dozens of photographs. The questions flowed from every direction, all via our interpreter and they flowed back - via our interpreter. She was going to be busy for the next few days!

We were taken directly from the press room to the waiting coach, missing completely the rigid customs and immigration process the rest of our party had endured. Our coach took us through the streets of dark Havana to the Hotel National. A very old building, the Hotel looked as if it could do with a facelift. It was big and imposing but the one lift failed to be adequate. Large queues built up as the stairways were closed off.

I booked into my room with Roy Huddleston. It was now around midnight and we had been invited down to an evening meal. We had reserved tables in the cabaret room and as I sat down amongst my own friends, our interpreter insisted I sat with the Cuban delegation on their table. It wasn't very interesting as the only person who could speak English was our lady friend, the interpreter - or so I thought.

The cabaret was just like any other cabaret, conversation was getting rather limited, the Cuban gentlemen were talking amongst themselves and giving me an occasional smile. I started asking the interpreter about Cuban people. Who were these people on our table, what did they do? The answers were very guarded. Then suddenly the gentleman who was sitting next to me and hadn't said a word to me all night, suddenly turned to me and said "Is everything alright with you?" I replied "yes, fine thanks". Then I froze. I thought they couldn't understand English. They must have been listening to everything I was saying pretending not to understand a word. So, this was Cuba. I tried to be a friendly guest. I am quite well known for being rather fussy about what I eat. Something was served to me that tasted vile, it was the worst tasting dish I have ever had. My new Cuban friend turned to me "Good, yes?" "Great," I replied, not daring to admit what it really tasted like. Forcing it down was agony. I learned later that everyone else had left theirs, but glasses of unusual tasting Coke helped to clear the taste.

Although it was now around 2.00 a.m. a few of us couldn't resist a short walk outside our Hotel. Incredibly there were lots of people walking about, buses and trams were full. We just couldn't believe that so many people were up and about at that time. They must have been coming and going from work, certainly not from discos or nightclubs.

Our first full day in Havana, Cuba, started with a breakfast of cheese and ham sandwiches followed by a cheese and ham sandwich. I don't remember eating anything else in the Hotel during the whole time we were there. After breakfast - at least I think that is what it was supposed to be - we were taken on a sightseeing tour. New housing estates, new factories, in fact we were taken to all the places they wanted us to see and spoke of nothing else but the new revolution and how everybody was working to put the country on its feet again.

The normal shops in Havana were out of bounds to the tourists. Most things for the locals were on ration. Two pairs of trousers a year was typical of the desperate shortage of clothing. Most foods were basic and the thought of ration books take us back to the Second World War.

Despite these shortages, I felt safer in Cuba than in Haiti. Although living standards are pretty low, they still seemed much higher than in Haiti. We were taken to what was called a duty-free shop in Havana where presents still appeared expensive, but it was good to buy some Havana cigars from Havana.

We returned to our Hotel, one of the best in Havana, for lunch. Guess what we had? There was an attractive swimming pool area and we relaxed in the afternoon before the big game.

As I've mentioned before we had two goalkeepers on this trip: Keith Jones and Roy Davies. Both of them had injuries prior to the game and it was arranged that they went to special clinics for treatment. Both of them were amazed at the modem equipment that was available to them.

Cuba has a lot of problems, but one problem it doesn't have is in providing every conceivable sport and stadia for the public. Intersport are in control of all sport in Cuba and everywhere in Havana were stadiums and areas of every shape and size catering for every sport. It is understandable why Cuba and other communist countries do so well in sport, especially at the Olympic Games.

We were taken to the stadium for what was going to turn out to be the biggest game we had ever played. We were the first English soccer club ever to play in Cuba at amateur or professional level. To this day Manchester AFC created history on 27th June 1975 by being the first and only team from England to play on Cuban soil.

Our coach arrived at the Stadium Latin Americana and we were amazed to find that the stadium which usually housed baseball had in the centre of the pitch a dirt track. That was going to make it so difficult for the players running on grass and then suddenly finding themselves moving on something entirely different.

Otherwise the stadium was magnificent. They said that this was a bigger and nicer stadium than the one where soccer was usually played. The dressing rooms were big and I gasped when on a large table in the corner were heaps of fruit, enough to feed an army. After the diet of cheese and ham sandwiches and with temperatures in the early evening still in the mid-nineties, it was a most welcome sight.

Our opposition that night was none other than the Cuban National team. They were in the middle of preparing themselves for the Olympic Games in Canada and they thought that they would sharpen their claws against our touring side.

We were preparing ourselves for the game when I suddenly broke out into a cold sweat. The trophy that we always present to the opposing team before the game had been left in the Hotel. I dashed out of the dressing room and managed to get Jean Bateman to be driven back to the Hotel by one of the Cuban Intersport officials. I prayed she would get back before the game started.

The match was scheduled for an 8.30 p.m. kick off and half an hour before, both teams went out to parade round the ground, each carrying the other's national flag. Our captain, Wally Roberts, must have felt very proud. The crowd was building up and it was later recorded at 25,000. It was as the two teams were kicking in that our trophy arrived at the ground. As someone who is very keen on organising, it is annoying when something so important is forgotten. The two national anthems were played and it was so noticeable that you could have heard a pin drop, even whilst they were playing ours. That was very moving.

Before this visit few people had heard the strength of Cuban football. They were one of those unknown football countries who were taken for granted as being no-hopers. People only know of Cuba as the communist Caribbean island off the coast of North America run by Fidel Castro.

In the first minute of the game, our fullback, David Charlton, was given ten yards start by the Cuban winger and was left gasping as the winger caught up and raced away from him. After three minutes a shot from 20 yards rocketed past Keith Jones into our net, knocking his fingers back and leaving him wondering how he failed to get near a shot that he thought he saw all the way.

That was the start of a performance from the Cubans that left us wondering why we hadn't heard more about them. True we were jaded after a tremendous holiday, a lot of travelling, a very hot, humid evening and tummies full of cheese and ham sandwiches; however, we battled on but at half time we were 4-0 down.

The fruit in our dressing room was most welcome but as Wally Roberts gave vent to his feelings he failed to see a Cuban TV cameraman who had walked into our dressing room and recorded his every word and reactions. Certainly, the Cuban people will know that we take the game very seriously.

The second half continued where the first left off with the Cuban forwards baring down on our goal. Keith Jones had coped well with the pressure but his injuries were now showing so I replaced him with the only half fit Roy Davies.

Roy had been on the pitch only a few minutes when Cuba were awarded a penalty. Not the best preparation for any goalkeeper let alone a substitute one so early.

Roy takes up the story: "I stood waiting on the goal line after having received some good advice from Fred Eyre. After watching the way the Cubans could hit the ball so hard, I decided to dive to my right. As the player ran up to take the kick I dived instinctively and as I lay there on the ground I suddenly realised that the ball was under my grasp. The crowd were cheering wildly. I jumped up for joy thinking I had saved the penalty. Then our centre half Bernard Peavoy told me that the ball had gone into the net and as it bounced out again, I had caught it!"

The Cubans scored again and with just a few minutes left, Bernard Peavoy went down injured. Our trainer Dave Jones hurried onto the pitch, only to be given the red card by the referee for not getting his permission to come onto the field. Bernard was finally carried off as we remonstrated with the referee. At least Dave holds the distinction of being the only Englishman to get sent off in Cuba!

The players were shattered. They had given their all against a team who one year later in the Olympic Games in Canada fought a 0-0 draw against Poland. That Polish side was their strongest National team including Kazio Deyna and all the big stars. That was the standard of the Cuban side, so the 6-0 result was not that bad against all the odds.

The Cuban TV interviewer after the game seemed to be mainly concerned with what my thoughts were on the Cuban side. "I thought they were disciplined, skilful and very fit", I replied.

The players made their way wearily back to the Hotel. On arrival around midnight we were told that we had to leave the Hotel at 5.00 in the morning to catch our flight back to Jamaica. The Cuban authorities had brought our departure forward as the King of Sweden was arriving in Havana and they wanted the airport cleared.

It was a bleary-eyed party that left Cuba behind to make our way back to Kingston. As we flew over the Cuban coastline, my thoughts went back to the days when I thought that to see the coast of Northern France was to fulfil all my dreams. Now here we were, the first and only English soccer side to have played in Cuba. We were leaving behind a wealth of memories but taking with us an experience and some cigars that our men in Havana will always remember.

We had almost a day to kill before we made our way home. We decided to make our way to a small Hotel owned by some Canadians who had provided the after-match buffet and entertainment after our earlier game in Kingston.

The ten-hour flight back to London proved very tedious and added to that a ten hour wait in Kingston airport as our plane was delayed, it was a very tired party that arrived back in England. We missed our flight connection to Manchester so travelled on the midnight train, arriving home at 4.00 in the morning.

Tired we were, but looking back on this holiday, it was every bit as good and exciting as I had hoped it would be. It was worth every minute it had taken to organise and it kept the adrenalin flowing for a similar repeat the following year.

Keith Jones pushes a shot past the post in Cuba in 1975.

The Stadium Latinoamericano welcomes the two teams.

11

Pele signs for us

On the Monday morning I should have been back in the office, but as soon as I arrived home I felt terrible. For the first and so far, the only time in my life I got jet lag and I didn't enjoy that one little bit. I spent all day in bed recovering. Early on the Monday evening and feeling a little better, I answered my bedside telephone. It was a lad called David Briody. I had recently got to know him and he was going to play quite a big part in my life.

At the time he was just a young lad who ran a team called Mancunian, but for someone of his tender years he had an insatiable appetite for administration. Usually a lad around 20 years of age just wants to play football but Dave was different. He loved organising and he dreamed of becoming Secretary of a Football League Club.

He also had that ambitious streak as I have, of taking his football team abroad. He was very interested in our trip and was keen to know how we went on. Dave will enter this story again later.

Grasmere Rovers were still going strong, but we weren't winning many honours. My thoughts were still wrapped up in those foreign tours and after our Caribbean carnival, a map of the world was my regular companion. In all these years with Grasmere, I had been the manager of the club. The usual endless amount of jobs, getting players to the ground and picking the team. I decided it was time to pass my problems on to somebody else.

A good friend of mine who was Secretary of the Manchester and District League, Peter Hollins, was keen to have a go and I was just as keen to hand over. Peter was an Insurance Broker with his own office in Blackburn. It was good to step down and give a little more thought to our next overseas journey.

The Caribbean had been so good that we just had to return to the area. The next venue was Nassau in The Bahamas and just across the water was the coast of my next goal - North America. We had ventured into Russia, into Cuba and into Africa so it was about time that the United States took some stick from our touring party.

Again, there was no problem in filling places for this tour. The 30 places filled in no time with lots of the old favourites coming along, i.e. Fred Eyre, Dave Brooks, Stewart Drummond, Wally Roberts, Tim Ingham and Dave Briody.

In Nassau we stayed in some luxury apartments and I arranged a three day stay in Miami in a Hotel on Biscayne Boulevard. Football in the Bahamas - yes, they do play football in the Bahamas - was arranged with three games against their National side, their League champions with the fascinating name of Nick's Bodyshop, and the Cup Winners, St. Georges.

We did well in the games. Obviously, the standard wasn't up to previous years, but we drew 1-1 against the National side and beat both their League teams 2-1. All the games were played in the Elizabethan Stadium which had quite a good playing surface.

The only black mark I can put against Bahamas football is their lack of organising ability. For our first game against Nick's Bodyshop we turned up at the Stadium one hour before kick-off time to find the ground closed and nobody in sight. With only fifteen minutes to kick off time somebody decided to open up and nobody seemed too bothered when we kicked off half an hour late.

Despite their casualness it was very interesting at a reception held by the Bahamas FA in a Nassau hotel to hear how keen they were on soccer. They have just eight League sides and speaking to one of their referees it was enlightening to hear how enthusiastic he was for Bahamas soccer.

Wherever one goes in the world, soccer is played and the locals are as keen on their side as the next person. Soccer in the Bahamas had been helped by some English people being involved. One such person was Eddie Raynor who did a lot to help us enjoy our games on this beautiful island.

The Bahamas conjures a turquoise sea, fine white sand, a hot sun and swaying palm trees. We weren't disappointed. It had all those features and more besides. The only drawback was that it is an expensive place. They have a system that people receive tax free pay but all the goods bought in the shops include tax. That makes items very expensive for tourists.

A bridge spans Nassau and the Atlantic to Paradise Island. What an aptly named place that was. I managed to keep up my record of not losing any money in a Casino by walking out winning one dollar. The very last of the big spenders!

The beach outside our apartments was absolutely gorgeous. In the distance we could see a small uninhabited island where the Beatles made their "Help" film. One day we hired a motor boat and whilst Geoff Goodwin was good at water skiing it was great fun watching John Godfrey, Tim Ingham and Mike Hackney flopping into the sea.

Despite my love for the Bahamas or as Dave Briody called it, the "Ban-ya-mas", we looked forward to our visit to Miami.

This was in 1976 when Miami wasn't open to British visitors as much as it is today. It was a short 90-mile flight to Miami and I was very excited as we flew into this sprawling city. Looking down on the Florida skyline, my first glance of North America took in a familiar sight, a twisting maze of motorways, or should I have called them freeways - and turnpikes. I knew we were now in America.

I was impressed with my first visit to Miami although I have been back since and was disappointed. The first visit brought one particular surprise, my first view of the famed Miami beach. After the beautiful beaches of the Caribbean and the Bahamas it was no better than Blackpool prom.

In charge of our football on this tour was Dave McCormack. A very popular person, Dave is a fully qualified FA coach. He has been sent to various parts of the world coaching and his training sessions on the holiday went a long way to providing us with a well organised team.

I arranged to contact a gentleman named Andy Henry in Miami who was the President of the Florida Soccer League. He arranged a tournament to coincide with our visit and we found ourselves in a multi-national bonanza with immigrants living in Miami representing teams from Haiti, Peru and British Honduras.

We played the Peruvians in the first game in temperatures around 100 degrees. Not very pleasant! We lost 2-1 and had to be satisfied with the game for third or fourth place the following day. We won that one 3-2 against the team representing British Honduras and felt very satisfied that we had at least won a game.

We only had a three day stay in Miami before returning to The Bahamas, but I liked what I saw. One night a few of us visited probably the most famous hotel in Miami, the Fontainbleau. With the help of John Godfrey we got ourselves mixed up in a national teachers' convention and spent a very interesting night with people who were so friendly and made us feel very welcome.

One point has always struck me with the Americans: when they do something, they do it properly. Nothing is done in half measures. Dave McCormack and I decided to spend a few hours in The Parrott Jungle. Now doesn't that sound boring? Nothing of the sort. We spent a fascinating three hours exploring spacious grounds with all kinds of bird life and plant life laid out in beautiful gardens.

As we left North America I vowed that I would return as soon as possible.

The football had been quite successful on this trip but of course the standard of opposition hadn't been as high as, for example, the previous year in Haiti and Cuba. It was good to play against teams of a similar standard to ourselves, but that big match atmosphere had been missing; small grounds and only a few hundred spectators in contrast to the big stadiums and thousands of people.

Some of the players who didn't come on the Jamaica trip but had heard of the big matches that we had, must have been slightly disappointed at the smaller games on this trip. However, they were still enjoyable but it is impossible to arrange big games in every country every year.

That urge to return to The States was the basis of our next trip in 1977 to Niagara Falls in Canada and New York. A trip which produced a thousand and one problems but also turned out to be an unforgettable journey.

We flew on a CP Air Jumbo from Manchester to Toronto with a party of 33 people. From Toronto we completed the 90-mile journey to Niagara Falls by motor coach. We stayed in a Motel that was very comfortable with accommodation only.

I will always remember my first view of Niagara Falls. It was breath-taking. Without doubt one of the best experiences of my life. There are two different Falls, the smaller American Falls and then the gigantic Horseshoe Falls which are in Canada. Standing on the Canadian side and looking across the river it is only around 100 yards to the United States. The Rainbow Bridge connects the two giant countries.

To the right are the Canadian Falls that are shaped like a horseshoe and are throwing 155 million litres of water a minute into the gorge below. It is an awe-inspiring sight with several ways that people can get a very close view and even get wet as the spray forms a mist. There is a boat trip on "The Maid of the Mist" but first of all you have to don your Wellies and waterproof garments.

It is difficult to understand how the little boat isn't torn in half as it bobs about only feet away from the roaring whirlpool, rapids and the Falls themselves. A walk amongst the beautiful gardens overlooking the falls goes to a point where people can lean over and put their hands into the water seconds before it cascades over the top. A skylon hundreds of feet high gives a tremendous view of the whole area around the Falls.

There are plenty of parks and lots of attractions in the town. We spent a very enjoyable week in Niagara, certainly an experience

I shall never forget.

That was only one experience, however, for so much happened on this holiday that there was hardly any time to sleep. More about that a little later as the football side of the trip was overall a resounding success.

Our first game was in Kitchener where we were playing an Ontario State XI, which was almost the Canadian National team. The game drew a record crowd of just over 2,000 people to a soccer game in Kitchener. The captain of the National team, Jim Douglas, was in the side and making a special guest appearance was Brazilian World Cup star, Marinho.

He only played for ten minutes before he disappeared down the tunnel which would have pleased his marker, Fred Eyre. Or as Fred put it, "I marked him so tight he couldn't stand anymore, so he walked off!"

The game was presented to the crowd in a typical American style with each player being introduced to the crowd individually and the Lord Mayor kicking off. The Canadian and English National anthems were played and it is when we are thousands of miles from home that our anthem suddenly makes us feel very patriotic and proud to be British. The realisation is that the anthem is being played because we are there and it brings a tingle down the spine every time I hear it played in a foreign country.

We were again surprised at the standard of football in a country that isn't really renowned for its soccer, but they gave us a few surprises and we lost 6-3. Not a very good debut for manager Pete Hollins, he was soon to learn that playing football in a foreign country was an entirely different ball game.

At the reception after the game Roy Davies announced his engagement to Lorna so that cheered everybody up after our disappointing performance.

Our second game was against Niagara Town and we again disappointed against a very ordinary side in drawing 3-3. The Canadians, we were beginning to find out were very friendly people and we received lots of invites to local parties.

Several sides wanted to play against us and every time I returned to the Motel there were a stack of telephone calls. I have never known so many queries with people wanting to get in touch.

Then there was the problem of having to get Visas to go into the United States for two of our party. They didn't have time to get them in England so I took them to the American Embassy in Toronto.

What a problem that was. One whole day trying to persuade a nasty faced Embassy official that we were only travelling to New York to play soccer. No way would he give them Visas. We made our way back to Niagara sadly reflecting that we would be two members short going into America. Many- telephone calls produced no luck.

I decided that I would take a risk and hope that when we reached the border the customs officials would let us all through. It worked a treat. Thirty-one people with Visas and two without crossed the border into America thanks to a kind immigration official. Amazing after all the trouble we went to in the first place.

During this trip we had one major problem, a family called the Armstrongs. After our games in Canada we had to travel around 500 miles to New York via a place called Syracuse. How we were to get to these places from Niagara Falls was the big talking point. The cost of travel was extra to what we had already paid and some people couldn't afford even to travel by Greyhound bus. The Armstrongs in particular were rather short of money.

One day Mr. Armstrong told me he had found the perfect way to travel into the States. We could hire our own bus and he would drive it for us. We held a meeting - the first of many -and decided rather reluctantly that this was how we would go.

It was only when we saw the bus that we realised what we had let ourselves in for. It was old - very old - and had wooden seats and no luggage compartment. The thought of driving 500 miles in that old bus, sat on wooden seats with luggage piled up high inside, was not my idea of what these holidays were all about. On the side of the bus was the most inappropriate sign imaginable - "Honeymoon Special".

Fred Eyre's face told its own story but being 'the good team man' he is, he scrambled with the rest of us into the bus for the first stage of our journey to Syracuse. Mr. Armstrong, our willing driver, drove us through customs on Rainbow Bridge into America and we rattled our way at a very steady 30 miles an hour towards Syracuse.

We eventually arrived at our Hotel, the Holiday Inn, and gratefully eased ourselves into comfortable rooms. Mr. Armstrong parked his bus, hopefully somewhere out of sight, and our thoughts and attention turned to the big game the following night.

As a place, Syracuse was rather drab, but our hotel was more than adequate. It must have been around 1.00 a.m. that I met Mr. Armstrong in the hotel corridor. At the top of his voice he announced that he refused to drive the bus into New York. I didn't know whether to laugh or cry. Doors opened as people wondered what was going on. Mr. Armstrong did have a habit of telling the world all his problems.

What the reason was, nobody could find out, but here we were, still 250 miles from New York with a bus nobody could drive and left with the problem of what to do next. We held a meeting at 1.30 a.m. and deferred our decision to another meeting. We had a game to play that night and Peter Hollins was concerned at team morale.

The game was against Scuderi Syracuse who were champions of the New York State League, but despite the uncertainty during the day and the doubt as to whether we would play in New York, the lads turned on a magnificent performance. Goals from Lee Farrar, Kelvin Armstrong and Fred Eyre gave us a 3-0 victory.

This was a very enjoyable game. Played under floodlights with a good crowd watching and a visit from the local TV station, all our problems seemed miles away. The Armstrong's had the cheek to turn up at the after-match reception so I decided to be tough. In no uncertain words they were told to take the bus back to Niagara and we would carry on to New York under our own steam. On reflection, "Honeymoon Special" would have brought New York to a standstill!

I was up all night as I discussed the events with Dave Briody and made many telephone calls to find ways and means to reach New York. There were only so many seats available on certain 'aircraft and the Greyhound coach service.

Believe it or not, we held yet another meeting at 6.30 in the morning and organised ourselves as to who went by what. I lost count of the number of meetings we had.

It was a five-hour coach trip to New York or just under one hour by plane. I went by coach this time and couldn't help feeling excited as we reached the skyline of this amazing city. We had gone to a lot of trouble to reach New York but it wasn't just the skyline that attracted us to this metropolis.

I had managed to get a game organised against the reserve side of New York Cosmos in their Giants Stadium. The Cosmos at this time were being talked about all over the world. They had some Brazilian chap playing for them called Pele and West German Beckenbaur was also gracefully showing an appreciative American audience his skills.

Crowds of over 70,000 were regularly attending the home matches and soccer in the States had suddenly become alive. Unluckily for us the Cosmos first team were away in Los Angeles so we were unable to meet the great Pele. However, the pennant presented to our club from the Cosmos had the following hand-written message:

"Good luck to Manchester AFC, Pele".

That pennant will be treasured for the rest of my life. As we approached the Giants Stadium in New Jersey for the game my mind went back to when we played in Barcelona. We had come a long way since those early days, but the sight of such an impressive stadium made those early traumas all worthwhile.

The Giants Stadium is beautiful, clean, modern and typically American where everything seemed so big. The changing rooms were massive. Peter Hollins would need a megaphone to deliver his team talk! There were cubicles for each player to change and there was a rush to reach Pele's No. 10 first. It must have been the only race that Fred Eyre ever won!

The big attraction, however, was the playing surface, which was Astroturf. Generally, the players enjoyed the experience of playing on it. The ball ran true, although it did bounce unusually high. Players, too, were sceptical of falling as the turf did tend to burn.

We played a Cosmos reserve side that included former Everton and Northern Ireland player, Dave Clements and Aston Villa fullback Charlie Aitken. We played well but lost 6-1. It always hurts to lose any football game, but this score gave a totally wrong concept of the game. Harry Bowell scored our goal.

The game was played in an empty stadium. The authorities said that to open the ground to the public would cost them over 10,000 dollars for security. The electronic scoreboard flashed a message to us - "The Cosmos welcome Manchester AFC". We felt very welcome and very honoured to have played a top club in such a superb stadium.

Our hotel was situated on Broadway in Times Square, right amongst all the excitement in this most cosmopolitan city. I came across an amusing conversation in the lounge of the hotel as we were being allocated our rooms. Keith Bateman's wife, Jean, had been used to the best of everything and when she heard Roy Davies say that his and Lorna's room had 'Persian rugs' she couldn't help but feel a little outdone. What Jean didn't realise is that Roy was using the Cockney rhyming slang for 'bugs'!

The following day we attempted to cram as much sightseeing as possible into our schedule. A few of us decided that the best way to see as much as possible in a short time was to go on a cruise up the Hudson River. This took us right around Manhattan, past the Statue of Liberty, and it was fascinating to see places that had previously seemed a million miles away.

We had a three-hour boat journey and this was followed by a walk to the Empire State Building. I had used all my film on the boat trip so I decided to make my own way back to the Hotel for more film. I walked past all kinds of people and enjoyed the stroll through the streets of New York. All this talk about don't walk in New York on your own. I must admit that I didn't give it too much thought and felt quite safe.

As I neared the Empire State Building and Fifth Avenue to link up with the rest of the party, I suddenly couldn't understand where the Empire State Building was. Although it is easy for any stranger to get lost in New York I had to ask somebody where the Building was. Apparently, I had walked straight past it without realising.

I must be the only person who ever got lost by walking right past one of the biggest buildings in the world!

The lift rises to the 84th floor before changing into a second lift that completes the journey to the top. The view was magnificent. We were lucky that it was a clear day and the whole of Manhattan Island presented a global view with the Hudson River where we had earlier sailed, surrounding the most famous island in the world.

A walk through Central Park and a visit to Tiffany's completed a crowded programme. The biggest disappointment was the failure to be able to get in to see Yul Brynner in "The King and I" on Broadway. That really would have been the icing on the cake.

We had reached New York. We had seen New York. Now we had to get out of New York and back to Toronto to connect with our flight home to Manchester. After our experiences in getting to New York, it meant, of course, another meeting. I have never known a trip like this where everyone ran out of money. Some people were generous enough to lend people money on their credit cards so that they could fly back to Toronto.

The Armstrongs meanwhile had made their way back from Syracuse to Niagara on the Honeymoon Special and we met up with them again at Toronto airport as we made our way back to Manchester. Mr. Armstrong seemed to be as noisy as ever.

So ended a holiday that brought more problems than any other, but on looking back there were a lot of good experiences. Niagara Falls was spectacular, New York was stupendous and the football was exciting.

12

A Caribbean cocktail

H ome again and almost immediately the thoughts turned to next year's holiday. A trend had now been set on long distance and exotic holidays and at this stage entered one of the greatest players the world of soccer has ever known — Bobby Charlton.

Bobby had become a Director of Halba Travel in Hale Barns. I had used them several times in previous years and it seemed logical that our overseas tours should be organised through someone who had an extensive knowledge of the travel world. What better than to organise our trips through someone who is the British ambassador in every corner of the footballing globe.

Bobby Charlton's football skills on the field are as well-known as he is for being a gentleman off the field. For someone who is at the top of the tree in his profession, he is perfectly reliable in everything he does. That nowadays speaks volumes. Bobby always likes to be on time and if he says that he will ring you back — he will.

Two stories come to mind that emphasise the respect people have for Bobby Charlton. The first was in Mexico. I shared a taxi with Brian Connor and as Brian and I babbled away in English the Mexican taxi driver suddenly turned around and said:

"You are from England?"

"Yes" we replied.

"Where are you from?

"Manchester", was the reply.

"Ah, Manchester, Bobby Charlton", replied an excited taxi driver. There we were over 5,000 miles from home and as soon as we mentioned the word Manchester the first person the taxi driver thought of was Bobby Charlton. No wonder he had just been voted Most Legendary Figure in World of Sport.

The second story concerns a reception that was being held after a tournament Dave Briody and I organised. We were at the Lymm Hotel halfway through a meal when I suddenly choked on my chicken. Bobby was sat next to me and asked what was wrong. I remembered that I had left the trophies we were presenting to the teams and referees in the boot of my car some twenty miles away. I had travelled to Lymm on the Glasgow Celtic team coach, leaving my car behind. Bobby was very re-assuring as I panicked, wondering what to do next. Have you noticed, I have a habit of forgetting trophies?

However, within seconds, Bobby's wife, Norma, quickly volunteered to drive back for the trophies. I will never forget that moment. It is proof that nothing is too much trouble for the Charlton's.

Talking about the tournament, what a performance that was. Dave Briody and I thought that it would be a good idea to organise an international tournament - to invite a couple of foreign sides to Manchester and include two local sides. They are very popular on the continent, but very rarely played in England.

I spoke to Bobby Charlton about it and he suggested that probably some of the professional youth teams would be interested. Dave wrote to all the top clubs, Real Madrid, Barcelona, Juventus and others. Most of them were already taking part in other tournaments but we managed to get Benfica, Sparta Rotterdam, Glasgow Celtic and Manchester United.

We were very excited at organising an event with such famous teams taking part. Dave and I worked very hard at thinking of everything that would make the tournament a success. Bobby was the Patron, I was the Chairman and Dave was the Secretary. We were helped by Keith Bateman, Graham Clifford, Tim

Ingham, Graham Briggs and Peter Hollins.

The teams were put up at top hotels and with the help of Noel White, staged the games on Altrincham's football ground. Everything was organised to the finest detail. Flags, national anthems and even a pipe band. We had promise of sponsorship from several people, but were badly let down, especially from a leading local newspaper and a top announcer on a local radio station.

Consequently, we had to rely on the crowds and they fell well below the breakeven point. Publicity is such an important part of any organised event, but we were unlucky to be sandwiched between the FA Cup Final in which Manchester United took part and the European Cup Final with Liverpool splashing the headlines.

Even so, the football and organisation went really well and in a good Final, Manchester United beat Celtic 2-1. Three of the referees that we chose for the tournament were on the Football League list - Neil Midgley, Peter Tildsley and Roger Dilkes. Peter had the semi- final between United and Benfica and was in the middle of a riot on the field as Benfica went mad over a decision. Peter can't have had many tougher games than that one.

Despite the financial loss involved Dave and I felt as though we had done a good job and would dearly have liked to repeat the event every year, but the financial guarantees were a big problem. We know that if we could have this guarantee then we would have had all the top European sides queuing up to enter. Again, we had proved that ambition has no bounds, but because certain people in the media had let us down, we dared not risk another financial embarrassment.

The sun was calling again and we were off to another dream, this time Barbados. It was difficult to stay away from the Caribbean. The memories of Jamaica lingered strongly. Of all the different parts of the world I have been fortunate enough to visit, the Caribbean is the most attractive. As on the previous two trips, I organised visits to other islands to vary the experience, and what an experience.

Trinidad was included in the itinerary with a finale on the Robinson Crusoe island of Tobago. In between, a few of us were to fly over to Caracas in Venezuela, South America. Games were arranged in Barbados, Trinidad and Tobago.

We travelled by Jumbo jet from London to Bridgetown, Barbados. We were to be met at the airport by officials of the Barbados Football Association. After the ten-hour flight we lazily made our way through the small airport lounge to find that no-one had bothered to turn up to meet us. I dashed from desk to desk only to be met by typically non-interested persons. Then just as my hopes of transport were at their lowest ebb, a convoy of cars arrived to pick us up.

I should have known after our experience in Jamaica and The Bahamas that the Caribbean people were always late. "Oh, what's all the rush, there's no hurry", Life is just one long doze. Perhaps the heat has something to do with it, for when it's always over 75 degrees there isn't the same desire to dash about. The Bajans, as the locals were called, are a much friendlier race than the Jamaicans. They understand that tourism is so important to their economy and they go out of their way to be friendly.

We stayed in luxury apartments and I again had Tim Ingham as my roommate. I've already mentioned how late Tim always is and he let me down again on this trip. We were all meeting at 5.00 a.m. in Stretford before we boarded our own coach for the journey down to Heathrow. At 5.00 a.m. everyone in the party was there eagerly anticipating another holiday of a lifetime - except Tim.

Our flight was leaving Heathrow at 11.45 a.m. so we couldn't leave it too late before leaving. At 5.10 a.m. I decided to ring his home in Bury, some 12 miles away, to see what time he had left. The phone rang and was answered - by Tim!

After waking up, he had fallen asleep again. We couldn't wait for him so he was told to make his own way to Heathrow so we could meet him there.

Half way down the M1 we were just leaving a service station area after having a snack when suddenly Tim's car screeched in front of us and a breathless Tim entered the coach. His car was later impounded by the police and had to be bailed out by his sister, Pat. It takes all types.

Tim really felt at home in Barbados where time wasn't important. How he managed to maintain efficiency in his business as an Advertising Executive, I don't know. Pity, because he's such a nice lad.

The pace in Barbados was slow and although I was disappointed at the lack of scenic splendour it is a beautiful island. The beaches are gorgeous, but the capital Bridgetown failed to inspire me. There's not enough charm, too few shops and it's a little scruffy.

The second day on the island and my cine camera decided not to function. I love taking a cine record of our trips so I quickly arranged to take the camera to Bridgetown. I will always remember that journey. Our apartments were five miles outside the capital and I went on my own in the local bus. One pure white man amongst the black locals. To say I felt very conspicuous as they all stared at me for the whole journey, is putting it mildly.

One of the best days we have ever had on holiday was when our whole party booked to go on the "Jolly Roger". This was a pirate boat that sailed along the coast with free rum punch and a barbeque all provided in the price. On the way back there was a disco where everybody danced with anybody. I have never seen Fred Eyre so jolly as he was on the" Jolly Roger"! Paul Wilson said at the time that it was the best day he had ever had in his life.

On this trip we had Bobby Smith with us who in his more illustrious playing days performed for Manchester United. He was the Manager of Swindon Town at the time where they had some memorable cup runs. He was also at Bury and Port Vale as manager.

Then there was Harry Bowell, who was automatically nicknamed Harry O but when he drank a full bottle of Pernod on the first day of the holiday he was quickly re-christened Harry Pernod! His claim to fame was scoring that goal against New York Cosmos.

Also, on the trip was Mike Turner who was later to have a spell as our manager. I liked Mike; he was a real character and a good talker. He sold sports equipment for a well-known supplier and he must have done well for he really had the gift of the gab. He played non-league soccer for Altrincham, Mossley and Hyde and we had the benefit of the end of his career.

Another member of the party was David Charlton who was one of our longest serving players. David toured North America with Manchester Boys but failed to break into the big time. He has been with us all over the world and is a great servant and friend.

I was finding it very difficult to finalise arrangements with the Barbados Football Association. We had two games organised on the island, but one fell through due to the unavailability of the only stadium on the island that was capable of staging the game. We were left with just one game against the Barbados National team.

The transport that was to take us from the apartments to the stadium finally arrived over 45 minutes late. I suppose we ought to have known, but at least Tim made it.

The game turned out to be an amazing case of missed chances. We lost 1-0 but I have never seen so many chances missed as we completely dominated the first half. Mike Turner and Harry Bowell should have had double figures between them but that ball wouldn't go over the goal line. The heat then started to take its toll and we wilted like flowers in a hot sun. Barbados usually take part in the early preliminary rounds of the World Cup, but they are so limited on such a small island to compete with the bigger countries in the CONCAEF group.

The next stage of our journey was down to the southernmost tip of the Caribbean, Trinidad. We flew into Port of Spain and were given a VIP welcome. The difference to Barbados was striking. The Trinidad FA were actually there when we arrived and we were taken to the VIP lounge. It was just as well that we had that comfort because the Customs and Immigration officials took nearly three hours to go through our passports.

They had recently had a shootout in the airport and they appeared to be making sure that we weren't English soccer hooligans. Trinidad isn't as beautiful as the other Caribbean islands and has a real mixture of so many different races. The capital Port of Spain is a teeming city with its main streets full of interesting people and shops.

Trinidad & Tobago Football Association

Patron :
**HIS EXCELLENCY
THE GOVERNOR-GENERAL**

President :
MR. KENNETH V. GALT

Hon. Secretary & Treasurer
JACK A. WARNER

(Founded in 1906)
Affiliated to the F.I.F.A.)
(Affiliated to the C.O.N.C.A.C.A.F.)
(Affiliated to the Football Association, England)

P.O. BOX 400
PORT-OF-SPAIN,
TRINIDAD, W.I.

Cable Address "TRAFA"

Phone — 35915
34251

23rd March, 1978.

Mr. Chris Davies,
33 Grasmere Avenue,
Heaton Chapel,
Stockport, SK4 5HU
England.

Sir,

Re your letter of 10th March, 1978 my Association wishes to confirm that plans are now being made for your Club to play two games against our National Championship Team, Defence Force, on July 1st, 1978 in Port of Spain and against either TECSA, Malvern or Point Fortin Civic Centre on July 2nd.

I have taken the liberty to write to the English F.A., enquiring about your Club's status. Looking forward to an enjoyable tour.

Yours sincerely,
T & T Football Association,

Jack A. Warner,
Hon. Secretary.

Letter from the Trinidad & Tobago FA signed by the secretary Jack Warner. Warner became a Vice President of FIFA and President of CONCACAF before resigning following corruption allegations also involving then FIFA president Sepp Blatter.

We had two games arranged during our visit against their top League clubs, but first the whole party was invited to a reception by the British Commissioner. We found this exciting and with everyone looking very smart we were all on our best behaviour as we met the notables from the Trinidad FA and the British representatives of Her Majesty's Government in Trinidad. The previous time we had been honoured with a reception like this was in Tangiers. Then, we had mint tea - this time it was chilled orange juice.

As I stood talking to the High Commissioner my mind went back to the beginning, the Manchester Parks pitches, long treks into Europe by train. Here we were, nearly six thousand miles away, just a few hundred miles from the South American continent. Yes, we had come a long way. I looked around and sensed a very happy and proud party as they chatted and accepted vol-aux-vents from the house waitresses.

Our first game on the island was down in Point Fortin against their local team. It was about 70 miles south of Port of Spain and we were herded like cattle into several cars that had all seen better days. I was lucky to travel in a reasonably good one but poor Fred was unlucky on the way back when his car broke down.

We arrived in Point Fortin after a bumpy journey and the temperature well over 100 degrees They had somehow timed the game to start at 4.00 p.m. The teams were introduced before the game to the new President of the Trinidad FA and as I looked around, wondered where all the crowd had come from. Point Fortin appeared to be only a small town, but the whole population had turned up to watch us fry in the sun.

We lost 3-1 and again it underlined the extreme difficulty of playing soccer in a hot country whilst on holiday. We were well treated by the local club before we made our way back to Port of Spain.

Our second game was on the following night in the capital city against the League champions, Defence Force. At least the game had an 8.00 p.m. kick-off, with a humid sweaty evening a poor substitute for a blazing hot sun.

We performed well here and despite conceding an early goal managed to get one back with ten minutes to go through Tim Ingham. Two minutes before this Peter Hollins was trying to substitute him as he carried an injury, but when he scored he jumped about like a two-year-old. There is nothing like a goal to make one forget about an injury.

Just as we were celebrating an honourable draw the home side grabbed the winner in the final few minutes. We were down again and as the sweat stained players slumped in the dressing room after the game it was difficult not to feel for the lads after they had given so much. Another defeat, but a score line rarely tells the real story of a drama in such difficult conditions.

After the game we went to the upside-down Hilton Hotel, so called because you enter the foyer on the top floor of the Hotel and take the lift down to your rooms.

We had a week of our holiday left and I had organised for our party to continue the tour on the Robinson Crusoe island of Tobago. The plan was for the last few days of the holiday to be spent on a peaceful desert island where the sleepy capital was called Scarborough and the beaches were amongst the finest in the world.

The underwater wonderland of Buccoo Reef with its dazzling coral gardens and rainbow-hued fish, the deserted beaches with tall palm trees that stretch out to meet the clear blue Caribbean offered a tremendous contrast to Trinidad.

This was the place I had dreamt of and couldn't wait to relax on this enchanting paradox of an island. First however, myself, Fred Eyre, Dave Brooks, his wife Carol, and two other friends, also called Brooks - John and Carol - decided that the opportunity of visiting nearby Venezuela in South America was too good to miss. We decided to spend three days in Caracas before re-joining the rest of the party for those last few days in idyllic Tobago. Unfortunately, those plans didn't quite work out.

We flew out of Port of Spain with my head again in a whirl of excitement. Another continent was looming towards us and as we approached Caracas I was sorry that I couldn't organise any football games in this oil glut of a country.

The introduction to Caracas is spectacular. The airport is linked to a super expressway that cost a huge fortune to build. The 13-mile journey into the capital city climbs high into the mountains, tunnelling through sheer rock, spanning ravines and as the city comes closer the stunning counter play of natural splendour and man-made practicality comes into view. What was a quick journey suddenly turned into a crawl as the biggest traffic jams I have ever seen loomed up in front of us. It was just unbelievable! In all directions traffic grounded to a halt, main roads, side streets, it looked as though all three million inhabitants had taken to the streets at the same time.

We stayed at the Caracas Hilton - only the best for the best! Venezuela was at the crossroads with its economy, the rich were contrasting with the poor. As one of the major oil producers, some people had got rich quick and the rise of Caracas made it one of the richest cities in South America. Petrol was at the ridiculous price of 7½p per gallon; no wonder there was so much traffic on the roads!

One morning we got into a taxi outside our hotel and half an hour later when we had only moved 100 yards, we decided to get out and walk! Despite these problems it was an enjoyable experience, the only disappointment being our limitations in being able to move about the city.

I looked forward to those final few days in tranquil Tobago. I couldn't wait to relax on those golden beaches and also to create another first. We had a game arranged against a Tobago Select XI and we were to be the first English soccer team to play on the island.

We flew back into Port of Spain and out again on a small propeller aircraft for the fifteen-minute journey to paradise. Our apartments were next door to the airport and it was a strange experience walking from the airport over the road to our secluded accommodation and a reunion with the rest of the party.

The day was Tuesday, the time, late afternoon. We had until Friday to enjoy the luxury of peaceful Tobago. I was met by Peter Hollins and the look on his face told me immediately that he wasn't greeting me with anything but bad news.

He had apparently received a telephone call from BWIA, the West Indian Airline to say that we had to leave Trinidad for home on Thursday. When I reminded him that we were booked to leave on Friday by British Airways and we had a game on Thursday night, Peter replied that the British Airways flight had been overbooked.

I was furious. We had done everything right, yet we were being driven off the island one day early. I stormed into my bedroom to be calmly informed by Fred Eyre that he had been told that some of the party had found beetles crawling around in their beds. A cold shiver ran down my spine. I would run a mile from any creepy crawlies and the thought of beetles running amok in my bed was the final straw.

It was not a pleasant evening. My thoughts were on action to be taken the following day with the two airlines. I didn't leave the hotel that night as my plans were worked out. Before I went to bed I checked under the sheets and there, lo and behold, was a beetle hurrying for cover. Fred was right. My own tan had suddenly disappeared as I turned white. For half an hour I checked, double checked and then re-checked the bed before I decided that the way was clear. It was not a good night's sleep.

The following day, the sun was shining. The turquoise blue sea shimmered and the palm trees swayed as I turned my back on paradise and arranged to spend as long as it was needed on the telephone to try and put matters right.

The first problem was the telephone. There were only a handful of lines from the island to the main island of Trinidad and they were invariably engaged. When I could finally get a line, there were so many people to ring.

I spent ALL day on the telephone and seemed to get nowhere. Thursday arrived and I had hardly seen the light of day, never mind anything of the island. Some of our party thought that we should catch the Thursday flight home. Others were willing to wait for any other arrangement that could be made. The Tobago Football Association needed an answer on the game that evening.

British Airways were not co-operative and time was running out. We would have to get the 1.15 p.m. flight to Trinidad if we were to catch the BWIA flight to London. It was all we could do as there was no guarantee of any other flight home. We quickly packed our bags and ran from the apartments over the road to the airport.

As we were walking out onto the tarmac only a few yards from the aircraft, there was suddenly an intercom announcement that there was a telephone call for Mr. Davies. I was sick and tired of telephones but ran back into the airport concourse to find out what the next problem was.

It was British Airways saying that they had arranged for us to fly out on Monday to New York on an Air India flight and- then a connection to London. It was too late. The game had been cancelled and all our luggage had now been ticketed to London on the BWIA flight.

I walked sadly back to the aircraft. 'It was waiting for me as its propellers roared and I reflected on the final days of the holiday. I had seen absolutely nothing of Tobago. Not even the pleasure of the scenery between the airport and hotel.

As our plane roared into the air it pulled away over the sea to deny me a final chance of seeing Tobago from the air. I just wasn't to see Tobago. The dreams of relaxing in lush tranquillity were not to be. I had been denied a dream I had stored for months. We had missed the opportunity of playing a historic game on this desert island. Months of planning had been shattered.

The more I look back on this holiday the more I believe that from a personal point of view it was the one I least enjoyed more than any other. Yet people who went still say that they had a fantastic time and really loved Barbados. It always pleases me to hear people say they have enjoyed holidays I have organised, but despite the places we visited, that holiday remains right at the bottom of my list.

I was more than ever determined that nothing was to go wrong again despite being aware of the fact that when the world is your oyster everything can go wrong at any time.

A plane lands over the road from our hotel in Tobago in 1977.

From Burnage to Barcelona - Chris Davies

13

Enter Uncle Albert

We arrived home to have an immediate change of manager. Peter Hollins stepped down to concentrate on his M & D job and we appointed Mike Turner. We hoped his experience would bring us some success.

The season passed very quickly and Mike found it increasingly difficult to find time in giving the team his full attentions. His job as a salesman with a leading sports manufacturer was taking more time than he thought and at the end of the season he resigned. Mike was a great character, a good talker - he could convince most people that black was white, but we were sorry to lose him.

We advertised the position and from six applicants chose an ex player called Albert Pike. That choice was to turn out to be the best move we have ever made. More about Albert and his successes later, but meanwhile - yes, another trip was being organised.

For the past few years we had ventured into exotic territory many thousands of miles away, but I thought we had to take a breather and come a little nearer home. I chose Cannes in the South of France and remembering my comments about avoiding things going wrong, made the usual meticulous arrangements before our departure. We had a small coach taking us down to Heathrow Airport. The first surprise was that Tim turned up on time! Then as we trundled down the M1 I began to worry that we were cutting it rather fine catching the 2.00 p.m. flight to Nice. When we got caught in traffic just before the M4 my bottle began to go!

At 1.15 p.m. we hadn't even reached the M4 and the traffic was thick in front of us. Perhaps the plane would be late, they usually were. Our goalkeeper, Bob Frais, jumped off the bus and asked a neighbour if we could use his phone. We had crawled another 50 yards as Bob caught us up to say that the flight was on time. Wasn't that just typical? When you wanted it to be late it had to be on time.

We finally arrived at Terminal Two at one minute to two. I dashed off the coach and rushed up to the desk clutching all the tickets. I was met to be told that the plane was on the runway just taking off. This was the first time I had ever missed a plane.

We finally had to go standby via Paris and arrived in Nice a little tired and weary and very late. We had travelled all round the world and yet a simple trip to France had caused all types of problems. I thought that Cannes was a marvellous place. A beautiful palm fringed promenade, open air restaurants and a good heady atmosphere. The whole coast is full of marvellous scenery, the weather was gorgeous. In fact, during the fortnight we were there I didn't see a single cloud. Fred Eyre had an inspiration to write his first book in Cannes and I can fully understand why.

We enjoyed Monte Carlo too and I managed to keep up my record when I won some money in the famous Casino. As we came out, the nearby Hotel Paris had collected a small audience outside. Apparently Frank Sinatra was inside talking to Prince Ranier. I wondered why I hadn't been invited into the discussions?

We had just the one game on this trip as we only had the bare eleven players. It was against the reserve side of French Second Division side Cannes and as Albert Pike gave his first team talk to our players, I hinted a note of caution in the tone of his voice. We hadn't got a very strong team with us and it seemed a case of keeping the score down more than going out to win.

As it turned out we won the game 1-0 with a Dave Charlton free kick rocketing into the back of the net. Dave's goal gave us our only 100% record on tour and was a great start to Albert's managerial career.

We were due to report at Nice airport at 7.30 a.m. for the flight back to England and it meant a 5.30 a.m. rise and shine. We had taxis booked to take us to the airport but when these didn't turn up I couldn't believe that we were going to have more problems. Apparently, there was a taxi strike in Cannes and again we missed the plane.

To be late for a plane once was remarkable, but twice on the same trip is downright incredible. We again went standby to Paris and then standby to London, finally arriving home in the early hours of the following morning. What turned out to be a simple nearby trip turned into another travelling nightmare. It only goes to prove that no matter how delicate and intense the arrangements, anything can go wrong at any time when travelling around the world.

When we finally got back, Albert was soon busy organising the forthcoming season as he gathered together the basis of a new team. We had to change grounds quite suddenly when Hyde United gave us very late notice to quit but we quickly maintained our standards when Glossop game to the rescue. The people at Glossop were kind and friendly and we enjoyed our association with them.

We also enjoyed that first year under Albert as we had our best season ever. The League was won by a record twelve points clear of the second team, only losing one game. We reached three Cup Finals and Albert had easily proved his value to the club. I was especially pleased for Dave Charlton and Norman Higginson; two players Albert had retained from the old team. They were two Grasmere stalwarts and it was good to see them part of a successful team.

This League championship put us into the Premier Division of the Manchester League, something that we had been aiming for a very long time. We had got there in style with a great bunch of lads. Foxy, Knighty, Batesy and 42-goal Peter Tilley, it had all been worthwhile waiting.

Albert Pike had played a good standard of semi-pro football and had been a hard-bitten centre half in his day. He had a very special way with players but was well respected. One game that season was a cup tie against his old club, Dukinfield Town. Albert wanted to win badly but it worked out rather difficult for him as the game was due to be played on his wedding day. As Albert was walking down the aisle with Sue, Grasmere were bearing down on the Dukinfield goal. We were leading 2-1 with five minutes to go and suddenly Albert appeared in the ground. He had grabbed Sue and crept away from the reception just so that he could see how we were going on. He was just in time to see Dukinfield awarded a penalty. Albert couldn't bear to look and as he walked away from the ground, missed a brilliant save from our goalkeeper, Stuart Dodd. The lads won that game just for Albert. Unfortunately, Albert passed away prematurely some years ago. He will be sadly missed and remembered with great affection..

During that season I tasted a nice little bonus with a trip to Milan with Manchester City. They had been drawn there in the European Cup Winners Cup and via City Director, Chris Muir, together with Fred Eyre and Dave Brooks, I travelled with the official party to Milan.

The San Siro was one big stadium I had so far not seen and it appeared as though I still wouldn't see it when we reached the ground. Thick fog swirled around the stadium and there was no chance of the game being played. It meant another night in Milan which I didn't mind and on waking the following morning found a brilliant sun shining through our window.

This game was played in the more illustrious days of Manchester City and they fought well for an honourable 2-2 draw. There were around 60,000 people in the San Siro stadium but they weren't as hostile as I thought they would be. Or so I thought. On leaving the stadium, some Milan fans decided to run wild and even the Italian police had problems in sorting them out. It was quite frightening at times as our coach ran the gauntlet and we finally raced clear to safety. Brian Kidd had scored one of the goals which gave me some personal satisfaction. I had met Kiddo before he made his debut for Manchester United and found him a likeable person. I followed his progress closely and was pleased that he did so well.

Albert with his trophy-winning team.

14

Down Mexico Way

A fter taking a breather in France I thought it was time to go further afield again. It was getting more difficult every year to find somewhere new that wouldn't be too expensive for the lads. After the usual deliberation I finally settled on one of the world's dream resorts - Acapulco.

Almost as quickly as announcing it the places were filled with 32 people. The holiday and football side took a lot of organising. The travelling was a little complex and the football took ages to finalise. It was, however, to provide us with the greatest experience we have ever had. I had heard that before League games in Mexico there was usually a minor game to entertain the crowd.

The world famous Aztec Stadium in Mexico City was host to four different League sides and I wondered whether it was possible to have a game in the Aztec before one of their big matches. I was lucky to contact Mr. Ruben Matturano who was staying in Manchester and had a friend who was an official of Cruz Azul, the top Mexican League side. He contacted him in Mexico and the wheels were set in motion to give us the footballing experience of a lifetime.

We left Gatwick airport and our Jumbo touched down in Dallas just at the time when the world was asking who killed J.R. We were to stop a few days in Dallas on the way home and people thought we might have found out some advance information. For the time being we left Dallas and its massive Fort Worth airport bound for magical Acapulco with a stop in Mexico City.

It was dark as we approached the Mexican capital and most of the party were feeling tired. I was wide awake however, as we circled possibly half a dozen times. I was fascinated by the view below with the flat city a kaleidoscope of lights.

Suddenly I could feel that we were about to land. Our 727 was making its run in to the runway below. We were approaching the ground. The lights were coming closer. I stared at the ground below as it came nearer by the second. Then just as we waited for the bump and the landing in another new country, the engines revved and with a scream the plane shot skywards and we were suddenly thousands of feet in the air again.

Apparently, we found out later that just as we were landing, another aircraft was on the runway and our pilot had taken avoiding action just in time. So, this was Mexico!

We landed a little later and much more smoothly in Acapulco. As we left our aircraft around midnight we were immediately hit by the humidity. It was a sticky heat and we couldn't wait to board our air-conditioned coach. On this particular coach trip, it was too dark to see the stunning scenery of the approach to Acapulco; future journeys made it the most stupendous view I have ever seen.

Winding down the mountain road from the airport the view towards the sea with the bays and hotels almost defies description. The very sound of Acapulco conjures magic, that scene was straight out of a magician's hat.

Our hotel was right on the beach with every room in the hotel having a sea view. Acapulco was beautiful, but we found the heat a problem. It was around 100 degrees every day, very humid with even the nights hot and sticky so it was a relief to go indoors to get cool.

The tourist part of Acapulco, with its fabulous hotels, hides the true Mexican way of life where the economy is struggling and there is a lot of poverty lurking in the hills. I shared a room with Dave Barrett and Brian Connor. I had not known Brian too well before but we instantly struck up a great friendship.

As we looked out of our bedroom window every day there was always a para glider smoothly flying by. It looked good, but it wasn't for me. One day as we lazed by the swimming pool, Vinny Crolla, Brian Simpson and Bernie Peavoy suggested that they should have a go at this flying craze. They persuaded me to go along with them. I wasn't very keen but thought that it might produce some fantastic pictures with my cine camera.

We walked along the beach and the first to get strapped in was Brian Simpson. When he came back ten minutes later his face was glowing and all he could say was "fantastic". Perhaps it wouldn't be too bad after all. Vinny and Bernie both went and came back saying the same thing. They all enjoyed the experience.

Now it was my turn. They put the straps around me as I stood on the beach, camera at the ready, and the speedboat that was to lift me high into the air, revved its engines.

Suddenly I jerked forward and found myself running down the beach. I gripped both sides of the strapping very tightly but realised that I could only grip one side as I had my cine camera in the other hand.

Then my feet left the ground and we climbed high into the sky. I pressed the button on my camera but it failed to work. I looked down at the sea below and sudden panic set in. My feet dangled in mid-air as I tried to get a grip of my senses. The camera was now becoming a hindrance as my sweaty hand tried to keep a hold and stop it from falling into the sea.

I was terrified. I shouted for help but nobody could hear me. I gripped the strapping with my left hand even tighter, although I would have been completely safe if I had let go. I swung through the air, shouting, screaming, my feet failing to find something solid below. We swung round on the return journey and I could see the roof of our hotel below me. Then again, my tummy did a nosedive as I remembered the instructions for landing. Above me on the right was a small lever I had to pull to get me down. How could I pull this lever when I was gripping the camera with my right hand?

There was nothing for it; I just had to pull that lever. Even though I could so smoothly have passed my camera to the left hand that gripped the straps, I just had the feeling that if I let go, I would plummet down onto the beach below. I quickly swapped my camera to the left hand and breathlessly pulled the lever.

I drifted earthwards and as my feet touched the sand I just crumpled into a heap. Brian said that in the ten minutes, I had lost all my sun tan. My face was as white as a sheet.

I have never been so frightened in all my life as I was during those minutes. All my previous fears of flying had returned. Whether it was the camera that had failed to record anything of the historic journey or whether it was the experience of my feet dangling in the air, I don't know. It certainly wasn't the height, but never again will I ever do any para gliding.

It took me some time to recover from that experience. I decided that those kinds of brave deeds should be left to the experts. Just as the famous diving from the cliffs of La Quebrada should be for those whose hearts are stronger than mine.

The diving is a spectacular sight. Usually made by young boys, they dive from a dizzy height into a sea below which is surrounded by dangerous looking rocks. Then they emerge victorious and run past the applauding crowd as they shower them with coins. Some people are to be applauded for doing dangerous things just for the kicks.

The heat continued to be a problem and I was beginning to wonder how we were going to fare in our first game against Acapulco. The time of kick off was 12 noon! The temperature only varied slightly at any time of the day and night, so I suppose midday was as good a time as any!

We lined up against Acapulco in the heat and glare of the midday sun with gallons of liquid refreshment on the touchline for the players. We had a good squad this particular year, with most of our successful side under Albert on the trip.

We had what I thought was an amazing result as goals from Harry Bowell and Micky Dewhurst gave us a fine 2-1 win. Every gallon of liquid was consumed. We have played football all over the world in heat, but this one in Acapulco was so far the hottest we had endured. Plans were now being made for us to travel to Mexico City and play a game in the Aztec Stadium against a team from Cruz Azul. Plenty of telephone calls were made to my contact there, Marco Dorantes, to finalise all the arrangements.

I had been fortunate to have Marco Dorantes at the other end of the telephone. He was the top referee in Mexico and was on the FIFA list. He had refereed Pele four times, once in the Aztec and the Giants Stadium in New York and twice in the Maracanã, Rio.

The excitement was mounting. Locals in Acapulco gasped when we told them that we were playing Cruz Azul. "You play Cruz Azul" they would say with eyes bulging.

I still couldn't believe it either. Until we actually kicked off it would remain as a faraway dream. I could imagine us playing in the stadium and then waking up to find that it really was a dream.

The day arrived when we were to travel to Mexico City. A one-hour flight and we were in the Mexican capital with a much smoother landing than the first time we had arrived. We were met by Marco and he immediately struck me as a most charming person.

Nothing seemed too much trouble for him. He was at the top of his profession in Mexico and was recognised everywhere he went. He owned a thriving sports business in the City and appeared to be one of the few people in Mexico who was making a lot of money.

We didn't see a lot of Mexico City in the time we were there as we had a second game arranged the day after we played in the Aztec and the sprawling city was difficult to cover.

Marco advised us not to go out alone but in large parties. Vinny Crolla wanted to buy a paper one morning and had to have an escort of seven people to go along with him. Despite that, we didn't see or sense any violence whilst we were in the place.

The one pleasing aspect in Mexico City was that it was appreciably cooler. The City is 7,600 feet above sea level and the biggest worry is playing football at such a high altitude, but nothing was going to stop us now from sampling the experience of a lifetime.

Never again!

Fred Eyre exchanges pennants with Dave Clements before our game with New York Cosmos in The Giamts Stadium in 1977.

Pennant from New York Cosmos to Manchester AFC signed by Pele.

The squad before the game in barbados in 1978

Manager Albert Pike with Roy Davies and son (right) and Dave Cockhill (left) with trophies.

Discussing tactics with John Alleyne, President of the Trinidad & Tobago FA in 1978

It's a winning team. This one was a great side under manager Albert Pike in 1978

Before the start of our game in the Aztec Stadium in 1980

Part of the 65,000 crowd in the Aztec Stadium 1980.

Christ the Redeemer, Rio, 1985.

What a view! On the way to Sugar Loaf Mountain, Rio, 1985.

Chris and Bobby Twiss with Ronnie Biggs on their way to the Maracana Stadium in 1985.

On top of Sugar Loaf Mountain in Rio. From left to right: Chris Davies, Nigel Freelove, Eddie Beresford and John Davies - minus cap - 1985.

In front of the Grand Palace in Bangkok. Sumo is on the left with Sunshine at the front in 1987.

Hope it's a box of chocolates! After the game in Delhi, 1988.

Some of the lads walk on to the Bridge on the River Kwai in 1988.

In Bangkok, 1988, from left to right: Ian Ward, Chris Davies, Gary Conner, Dave Charlton, Martin Briggs.

The The calm before the storm in the Nehru Stadium in the game against Mohun Bagan in New Delhi in 1988.

</150

Jairzinho demonstrates his skills at Park Road stadium in 1992.

Old friends. Mark Fitzgerald, Jean Harper and Ian Ward at a reunion dinner in 2001.

Great friends. Roy and Lorna Davies, who now live in Portugal. 50th reunion dinner in 2011.

Posing in front of the iconic Taj Mahal in 1988.

Chris with Sir Bobby Charlton in Lanzarote in 1986.

The C.F. Lloret side we played in 1968.

Top Spanish League club Elche with Asensi 2nd right on front row.

15

The Aztec Stadium

The morning of the game was cloudy, in fact just like a typical English day. The players also appeared cool as they quietly relaxed in the Hotel.

Our game was scheduled for a 2.30 p.m. kick off and we were to play a team comprising reserve players from Cruz Azul and to add a bit of spice, a sprinkling of ex Mexican Internationals. The game was to precede the main game which was a Mexican League match between rivals Cruz Azul and Atlanta.

At 12.30 p.m. the coach arrived at our hotel to take us to the Estadio Azteca. I went with Marco in his car and we went ahead of the team. We soon arrived at the ground and immediately the sheer size of the place stood out as we approached the official entrance.

Marco drove his car in through the big iron gates and down a long ramp at the back of the stadium. We got out of the car and walked forward to a large spiral staircase. We climbed the stairs and suddenly emerged into the daylight.

My heart missed a beat as I gaped at the most incredible sight in football. Only twice before had I had that same feeling of wonder. My first visit to Wembley Stadium and then my first sight of the Barcelona ground.

Both those however shaded into insignificance as I tried to take in the scene that lay before me. I had dreamt of how I thought the stadium would look, but the reality was one hundred times bigger and better.

By this time the rest of the party had arrived and the gasps that could be heard were in amazement at a magnificent stadium rather than the lack of air at altitude. I strode over the turf and thought of all the great footballers who had graced this showpiece of soccer. Pele immediately sprung to mind. Bobby Charlton had told me before we left Manchester that it was the best ground he had ever played.

The stadium has all seats and accommodates 110,000 people, some in private boxes, but everyone has a marvellous view of the game. The stands seem to reach out for the sky as the light filters through what appears to be a small opening in the ceiling.

Those early days on muddy, windy parks pitches in Manchester were a long way away. This was where football should be played. Our first ever game in 1961 against Alan Grafton's Mission Lads on a cinder pitch in Casson Street, Gorton, came into my mind as I walked back into our large changing rooms. In those early days we had changed in Alan Grafton's house and trotted over the road onto the pitch. Another room off our changing rooms in the Aztec led into a small chapel where teams could pray before the game if they wished.

I remembered the 1970 World Cup Final between Italy and Brazil played in this very stadium with the noise like thunder, the thousands of flags being waved all over the ground and the continuous chants from the Brazilian supporters of Bra...zil. What a tremendous sight and sound for any supporter.

As the players changed, I began to wonder and then worry how we were going to play. Would we let ourselves down and receive one of those heavy defeats that we had endured in the past? Or would we really perform on this world stage and show these Mexicans what we are really made of?

We were almost ready to go. Albert was giving one of his famous team talks and all the players looked eager for action. I went out ahead, ready to take cine photographs of the team coming onto the pitch and hopefully some good action shots of the game.

As I climbed the staircase and emerged again into the open behind the goals, I was hit by another incredible sight. The heavens had opened and some of the heaviest rain I have ever seen was absolutely belting down. I made a hurried retreat. My T-shirt with Manchester AFC blazoned across the front wasn't made to take that sort of weather.

I managed to borrow a raincoat from a ball boy and dashed into position, just in time to photograph our captain, Paul Knight, as he proudly led his team onto the pitch. The rain seemed to get heavier as the clouds opened, but it couldn't dampen our enthusiasm to get on with the game.

As we kicked off, the crowd were slowly coming into the stadium. I hoped it would build up to reasonable proportions to watch us perform so far from home. I noticed some supporters who were chanting our name and were told they were English people living in Mexico. It was good to see that we had support.

We were playing well, using the wide-open spaces and seeing plenty of the ball. The rain was slowly easing and the crowd were quickly filling up all those empty seats. The atmosphere was now beginning to build up and there were roars from the crowd as attacks were started and after 20 minutes, finished in great style by a Cruz Azul forward.

From fully 30 yards he saw that our goalkeeper, Stuart Dodd, had advanced a little too far and delicately "chipped him" to put us a goal behind. We weren't dismayed and a little later a good move ended with Mickey Dewhurst putting us on level terms.

Mickey was a very experienced player in Manchester but always carried a little too much weight. I remember him worrying before we came on tour as to how much he would sweat in the heat. As it turned out, I rated Mickey our best player on the tour.

Just before half time, Doddy was amazingly "chipped" again and we went in 2-1 down. Stuart is often reminded now that he must be the only goalkeeper to have been "chipped" twice in Mexico and he is six foot two tall!

When the players came out for the second half the rain had ceased and the crowd had grown to massive proportions. We were told that there were 65,000 people in the ground and the atmosphere during that second half was such that the players who took part will remember it for the rest of their lives.

The score remained 2-1 and although we lost the game, I thought that we had played well enough to deserve a draw. We received a great reception from the huge crowd as we left the field. A different reception than the one we received way back in 1961 as we made our way across Casson Street back into Alan Grafton's house. The score then was the same, a 2-1 defeat but the two games were worlds apart.

Perhaps in their own way, they were equally as important because if we had not played that first game in Casson Street and not replied to Alan Grafton's letter of "can my team play your team", then there would probably have been no Grasmere Rovers and most certainly no experience of a lifetime for a party of amateur footballers from Manchester in the Aztec Stadium.

We received a good press coverage the following morning and it was secretly a relief that we had put up a good performance. There were many photos taken of our experience. They will remain a very treasured memory of an unforgettable day.

The squad at the Aztec Stadium before the big game.

16

Into the frying pan

W e didn't have too much time to dwell on our experience in Mexico City, as the following day we had another game. Marco told us that it wasn't far, just in the suburbs. An hour and a half later we arrived to play the reserve side of Neza. It was a similar situation with the first team game following our match.

There was quite a contrast to the Aztec Stadium, but we now had to forget about that as one chance in a lifetime. This was down to earth and around 9,000 people saw us put up a jaded performance and go down 3-0.

The following day saw us take the flight back to Acapulco where we stayed for a few more days before making our way homewards via Dallas. We were feeling quite excited to be visiting a place that in England was making all the headlines. Who shot JR?

We landed in Dallas and made our way from the aircraft, through the corridor and into the airport. When we cleared customs, I told the rest of the party to stay where they were whilst I found out the whereabouts of our coach.

I hurried towards the sliding doors to walk outside the airport and as the doors parted and I went outside, I was suddenly stopped in my tracks. The heat was incredible, so much hotter than it had been in Acapulco. The temperature in the shade was recorded at 113 degrees whilst out in the sun it was a staggering 127 degrees. Texas was experiencing a heatwave that even Texans were finding difficult to cope with. People were dying because of the heat.

It was difficult to breathe as I finally found our bus. Then came the second shock - it wasn't air conditioned! The one difference from the heat of Acapulco was that in Dallas it was a dry heat. Even so, the best place was indoors and it was a relief to arrive at our hotel.

The thought of playing football in these conditions seemed a silly thing to do. The following morning Albert had all the players up early to do some training and in a cool 98 degrees they must have thought they were in a sauna. I stood watching under the shade of a tree and couldn't stand the heat any longer.

Soccer in Dallas was well organised at amateur level by an ex Englishman, Ron Griffiths, who ran several teams of all ages called Texas Longhorns. Our game was scheduled for a 6.30 p.m. kick off and in a temperature of 106 degrees, lost 2-1. Defeat in this game annoyed me. Playing against a team that on any other normal day we would have beaten quite easily we were further handicapped by inadequate refereeing.

Travelling the soccer world, one gets used to different interpretations of the laws and biased officials, but this one was the worst that we had ever encountered.

We only had a few days in Dallas, but despite the problems of the heat, I quite liked the people and was very impressed by the "class" of the place. Like many American cities it is a big sprawl with no town centre and it takes hours just to cross from one part of the city to the other.

The people were so friendly and it was difficult to understand when someone told me that the crime rate was amongst the highest in America. Even in "nice" places there are so many people who just have to do wrong.

Our stay in Dallas was too short, but we had an unexpected bonus. When we reached Dallas airport for the flight back to London, I was told that the flight had been cancelled. Flight 602 had been waiting to leave Gatwick. Passengers were queuing in the aisles waiting for the cleaners to do their job and the plane to be refuelled. The 400 passengers, however, had never taken their seats. For as the portable steps had been driven across the tarmac and up to the rear of the plane, a resounding crash was heard and a gaping hole had appeared in the fuselage. The hole was believed to have been made as the motorised steps were driven towards the airliner's rear door. It was an unfortunate mishap as the error of judgement was estimated to have cost Braniff Airlines over £1 million in damage and lost revenue.

We then had a further demonstration of the efficiency of American airlines. Within half an hour we were booked into the airport hotel, had a morning flight to New York and then booked the last seats on the evening flight out of New York direct to Manchester. After all the aggravation with flights in previous years, this was a superb piece of organisation and again proved to me that the Yanks know exactly what they are doing when it comes to sorting out any problems.

The delay worked out well as that evening, Dallas Tornadoes, who have now unfortunately gone bust, were at home to Tampa Bay Rowdies. That was too good an opportunity for Brian Connor and myself to miss. We drove by taxi out to the ground and witnessed our first North American soccer game.

The surface was Astroturf and the additional attraction was that the ex-Manchester United goalkeeper, Alex Stepney, was in the Dallas team. A lot has already been said on the style and presentation of American soccer. Even though the game was a boring 0-0 draw, it was still fascinating to hear all the gimmicks thrown at the crowd.

The commentator gave a steady stream of instant chat. The electronic scoreboard told us exactly when we had to cheer for the Tornadoes. Then there was that dreadful organ that built up to a crescendo when the Tornadoes attacked and then reversed into a sliding scale when the attack broke down.

The 0-0 draw did, however, give us the opportunity to witness at first hand the virtues of the penalty shoot-out. Alex Stepney made two fine saves to help his side to victory and I must admit that this different way of deciding a game has a lot going for it. The climax to the game was presented with an air of excitement as the skill required from the penalty taker and the goalkeeper is much greater than the conventional penalty kick.

On the referee's whistle the penalty taker has five seconds to score. He can do so by shooting immediately or dribbling the ball forward past the goalkeeper who is allowed to leave his goal and narrow the angle.

The Dallas stadium was big and spectacular so it was disappointing that there were only around 5,000 people present. The atmosphere, however, was totally different than the English game, with a vast majority of the crowd being young girls. Everyone seemed so friendly. At half time I went down for some drinks and my English accent was easily recognised. Immediately they wanted to know which part of England we were from and they ended a pleasant conversation by saying that they hoped we would enjoy the game.

Imagine receiving that kind of hospitality in England!

As we sat watching the second half of the game we became friendly with a family who were sat next to us and they offered to take us back to the hotel in their car. Their hospitality was unbelievable seeing that we were two strangers. Nothing was too much trouble for them.

After our game against Texas Longhorns we were invited back to the house of one of the players - the whole squad of 32! Needless to say, his house was big enough to cater for all of us, plus most of their side too. I believe his parents were out and unaware of our return but hospitality and friendship are top of the list when the Yanks have anything to do with it.

The following morning, we caught our flight to New York and for the people who had not been before; it was an added bonus to spend a day sightseeing before leaving on the flight home to Manchester.

Albert Pike and his wife, Sue, had missed the opportunity previously of going to the top of the Empire State Building. They were given an unexpected chance of doing so on this trip.

When Albert joined us he brought with him his assistant, Roy Venables. Roy ran our reserve side and immediately became a popular member of the club. His dry wit and humour is a vital part of any football team. Unfortunately, he developed food poisoning on this trip and spent a lot of the time in bed.

It is a pity when we travel so far and people pay a lot of money that they miss part of the holiday. The food generally in Acapulco was splendid and very reasonably priced too, so Roy was unlucky to fall fowl of the food!

Another popular member of many of our tours is Jimmy Hurst who does the best impression of John Arlott I have ever heard. "It's thirty-three for one and twenty to two on the big clock."

That was the end of another magic trip with a host of experiences behind us. The Aztec Stadium seemed a distant memory as we prepared for another English season. However, recalling the experiences of playing in probably the best stadium in the world hopefully will last forever in the minds of those who took part.

Team photo with the Texas Longhorns after the game.

17

The wonder of Disneyland

There are a lot of people who moan about too much football. Too much football on TV, too much football in the newspapers. "All you can talk about is football".

Football is a religion. The talking points that emerge are endless. The scandal about managers and players provide a continual stream of patter as events are discussed and some blown up out of all proportion. To people in the game, it provides an interest beyond the realms of fantasy.

Above all, it provides friendship. Life is all about making friends and football is the perfect foil for giving people an interest outside our mundane way of living.

Making friends is one of the most important things in the world. My years in the game have given me the opportunity of meeting all kinds of different people, many of whom are great friends, like Jean Harper who has travelled afar and is still a great friend today.

Many people have helped to provide my life with great friendship. There can't be anything wrong with football when it helps to bring so many people together.

The advent of world football and the access so easily to any part of the world has helped to spread this friendship to every corner of the globe. Improved telephone links and a love for football in every country in the world has helped to bring so many people closer together.

Don't knock this great game of football. It provides so much more than just the ninety minutes on the field.

After all the excitement of Acapulco and Mexico the following year provided a nice peaceful holiday in Fort Lauderdale, Florida. No problems, no worries, just sunshine all the way.

We jetted into Miami and then made the short journey to Fort Lauderdale. We had booked into some apartments which were right on the beach. This was my first meeting with Larry Gaffney with whom I shared an apartment: a skilful footballer who had a sweet left foot but lacked a bit of pace. I enjoyed his company for the two weeks and found that for someone who was only 21, he knew a lot about the administrative side of football.

My good friend, Brian Connor, was also on the trip, and it was good to see Dave Cockill and his family also enjoying the Florida sunshine. The longer we stayed in Florida, the more I loved the place. The people were so friendly. Everywhere people said "Have a nice day" and they meant it too.

We had two games during our stay and won them both fairly easily against College teams. In one game, Larry scored four goals, but it must be admitted that the standard of opposition wasn't as strong as on previous trips. Even so when playing abroad the conditions are usually worth two goals start to the home side.

This trip was more of a holiday rather than a football tour and we had a great time seeing all the local sights. The Everglades, Kennedy Space Centre and a journey on the Jungle Queen, but one trip turned out to be very extra special. That was the trip to Disneyland. Today this part of the world has become a massive tourist attraction, but when we visited in 1976 it was less commercialised and somewhere very special indeed.

It was the most exciting place that I have ever seen. There were 43 square miles of luxury resorts, with a host of outdoor sporting activities and in the centre of all this was the Magic Kingdom.

There were 45 attractions, over 70 shops and restaurants, musical groups playing everything from Dixieland jazz to country and western, plus of course Mickey Mouse, Donald Duck and all the other Disney characters. There was Main Street, USA, with double-decker buses and carriages depicting America as it was at the turn of the century.

There was Adventureland with the excitement of a jungle cruise and the pirates of the Caribbean. Onto Frontierland and the antics of the Country Bear Jamboree and a ride on the Big Thunder Mountain Railroad. The railway brought people face to face with swarming bats, a raging waterfall and a thunderous earthquake and landslide. There was the Liberty Square riverboat and the Hall of the Presidents.

Fantasyland had all the children's favourites with Peter Pan, Dumbo and Snow White and a fascinating voyage on a submarine 20,000 Leagues Under the Sea. Then there was Tomorrowland with its futuristic journey inside Space Mountain then a glide aboard the electro-magnetically powered Wedway Peoplemover.

Inside Disneyland there were magnificent hotels. There was the resort centre of Buena Vista. A cruise could be taken to Discovery Island where over 500 exotic birds lived amongst colourful flowers and trees with creatures like the Galapagos tortoise and Bald Eagle.

Those were just a few of the thousands of attractions in this wonderland. We drove our car from the hotel in Orlando and as we approached the road to Walt Disney Land a sign on the side of the road said "Tune your car radio to 1100 metres".

Rather puzzled we switched the radio from music to 1100 metres and suddenly a voice said "Welcome to Disney World! Just continue driving your car along this road". The voice continued to give us details of what to do and where to park our car. This was the first wonderment of Disneyland. We parked in the biggest car park I have ever seen, split into sections with names taken from all the Disney characters.

We parked in Pluto and almost immediately were met by a small railway engine pulling some trucks which took us to the monorail station. We were then taken to the entrance of the Magic Kingdom. The whole thing was totally futuristic! The efficiency and organisation was superb, typically American and the cleanliness was so effective that I'm sure if I had dropped a piece of paper on the floor, somebody would have been right behind me to pick it up.

The monorail I found fascinating. I had permission on one journey to travel in the driver's cab and took some exciting cine pictures from a dramatic angle. The monorail went around the complex of the Magic Kingdom and at one spot went straight into the foyer of the Contemporary Resort Hotel. The hotel was A-shaped and the sleek monorail glided out of the Grand Canyon Concourse to continue winding its way around the lagoon and to the other hotel, the Polynesian Village.

Over the years I have visited many countries and have been very fortunate to experience some tremendous scenes, stunning views and exciting trips, but the visit to Disney World provided the most fantastic two days of my life, with the exception of one hour on the first day when I went on some flying chairs with Larry and came off feeling as though the world had come to an end.

We took the opportunity whilst in Florida of seeing another North America soccer game when Fort Lauderdale played Toronto Blizzard. Although I again enjoyed the occasion it was sad seeing some of the world's great soccer names languishing in what can really only be described as obscurity. One such person was Gerd Muller and there were old stars from all over the world.

Before the game started each player was introduced individually to the crowd. Despite the presence of so many "names", Clyde Best, Jimmy Greenhough, Keith Weller, Cubilla of Peru and Holzenbeck from Holland, were just a few, the biggest cheer was for someone who really must be rated as an unknown, Ken Fogarty, who played for Stockport County and was born in Stretford. Perhaps there is a moral there somewhere?

When we arrived home my thoughts immediately turned to another event. In a few months' time, January 1982, it would be 21 years since Barrie Dean persuaded me to start a soccer team. A 21st anniversary Dinner was arranged at the Hotel Piccadilly and with the help of Dave Cockill and Gordon Ramshead we set about inviting as many people as possible who had been a part of the Grasmere scene at home and abroad over those years.

It was a grand affair with nostalgic moments meeting so many people who have helped to make my life so interesting. It was one of those nights where time moved far too quickly and nobody wanted it to end. It was a proud night for both myself and Graham Clifford who had been in it from the start. Two disappointments were that Frank Seymour couldn't come because he was ill and John McArdle, "The Duke" just didn't turn up.

At the end of the previous season we were shocked to learn that Albert Pike had decided to emigrate with his family to Canada and we would have to find a new manager for the team. We were sorry to lose Albert. He had done such a fine job for Grasmere Rovers. He had raised the standard of the club and we were all grateful for everything he had done for us.

When Albert had joined the club, one of the players he had brought to us was Jimmy Clark who had quite a bit of experience playing in a higher standard. Jimmy came from Glasgow and had played for Clydebank. We decided to offer him the manager's job on Albert's recommendation. He would have a difficult task following somebody who had been so successful.

18

East African safari

It was early in 1982 and the snow lay crisp and even. I was sitting in Bobby Charlton's office and we were talking as usual about exotic places. I had spent many months already wondering where our next trip was going to be but Bobby finally made up my mind.

For several years past Bobby had mentioned his love for Kenya in East Africa and he finally convinced me that Kenya was going to be the 21st tour I had organised. Bobby enthused over the place. "Without doubt the best place I have been to", he said. "Well, if it's good enough for Bobby Charlton then it's good enough for me", I thought.

Another exciting holiday was being planned but as was now becoming quite the usual thing with these long-distance trips, unforeseen circumstances intervened at the most unlikely times.

First of all, our plans to travel down to Heathrow were hit by a train strike and we travelled down by coach. After our previous experience of missing the plane, we left with plenty of time to spare. It was just as well for the coach developed a faulty tyre just outside London and we were thankful to a passing lorry driver for giving us assistance.

It was a long journey to Mombasa and we arrived in the early hours of the morning. The journey from the airport to the hotel opened our eyes as the locals strolled around in the hot sun, but despite the sparseness of the surroundings they seemed to have a happy smile on their faces.

I was so disappointed with Mombasa. Perhaps it sounds a magic place, but the town is very old and dirty and is not really very attractive. It is outside the town where the attractions are with a good standard of hotels on some beautiful beaches. The swimming pool complex in our hotel was probably one of the best I have seen.

The people in Kenya were the friendliest I have ever met. "Jambo", is what you would hear every time somebody walked past. That means "hello". The famous Masai tribe were to be seen everywhere and I found it very difficult to understand that they appeared to be living in a world that was a thousand years behind our times. They walked around with loincloths, carried spears and. lived in mud huts!

Amongst the Masai it is a tradition that a man is not a man until he has speared a lion face to face. The Masai in fact are more worried by cameras than by lions. They dislike being photographed, a superstition that says their soul becomes captured in the camera.

Kenya is a poor country and yet it was well off compared with the countries that border it: Uganda, Ethiopia, Somalia and Tanzania. More about Tanzania later, but I heard at first hand of the many problems that exist in Uganda.

I took a taxi from our hotel to the centre of Mombasa to sort out our air tickets for the homeward flight and I had a very interesting conversation with the taxi driver who had fled in terror from Uganda and was now exiled in Kenya. He painted a horrific picture of life in his homeland. Innocent people being killed not only in the Idi Amin regime, but in the present one too.

I have been fortunate to travel to many parts of the world and have been horrified to see so much poverty. On this trip to Kenya it struck home to me for the first time that probably around two thirds of the world are living on a much lower standard of living than we are. We seem to always want more and are constantly looking to improve our living standards, which is right of course, but we don't realise the millions upon millions of people all over the world living in poverty.

I have probably painted a grim picture so far which is really unfair. Here we were in Mombasa and everyone was enjoying themselves. The sun was shining; the palm trees wavered over a turquoise sea gently lapping onto a silvery, sandy beach.

Another disappointment on the trip was that we had an inexperienced team and there were some big football games lined up. Just to add fuel to those problems, as if by fate, one of our more experienced players - Gary Kirkwood - sprained his ankle whilst walking on the beach. Gary was on his first tour and had been so keen to play.

When I organise a long-distance trip one of the first things I do is to see which other country nearby we can visit. On this trip I managed to get in touch with the Tanzania Football Association and they arranged for us to play their top League side, Simba.

I was very worried playing against their top side with a weakened team, but several telephone conversations between Mombasa and Dar-es-Salaam failed to make them understand that we wanted to play a lesser team. When the tour was first organised, we had some good players in the squad, but some of these had to withdraw before our departure.

One other major problem also emerged during our telephone conversation. The Simba club wanted us to travel the 400 miles to Dar-es-Salaam by coach. An 800-mile round trip by road was absolutely out of the question. Our Tanzanian friend finally agreed that we would travel by air, but that then presented the next problem.

Unknown to me at the time, was the fact that the two countries of Tanzania and Kenya don't speak to each other. Not anything too serious like war, but just a diplomatic row which had closed the borders between the two countries.

The Tanzanians had to obtain Foreign Office permission from both countries to fly our special aeroplane between the two places. The telephone line between our hotel and Dar-es-Salaam was gradually becoming a "hot line". People we spoke to in Mombasa didn't believe that we were going to play football in Tanzania.

The telephone call from Dar-es-Salaam finally arrived, giving permission for our aircraft to land in Mombasa. I already felt another sense of achievement and began to get excited as another new country loomed on the horizon.

We were then told the staggering news that this would be the first aircraft to land in Kenya from Tanzania for five years. The game of football had broken another barrier although unfortunately it was only a temporary one.

We arrived at Mombasa airport and were told rather sarcastically at the check-in desk that there was no aircraft arriving from Tanzania and it was unlikely that there ever would be one arriving.

I wondered whether we were being led into a hoax. Perhaps the Kenyan authorities had prevented the aircraft from landing. I dashed up the stone steps to the viewing veranda and failed to see an aircraft labelled Air Tanzania. The Kenyan authorities were not very helpful. We didn't have any tickets to prove that the flight was genuine. I had been told that these would arrive from Tanzania with the aircraft.

Half an hour passed by with my bottle beginning to go again. Then came the casual message that our aircraft would be landing in ten minutes. The relief was tremendous. I was smiling again.

It was only a small aircraft, a Fokker Friendship of Air Tanzania with a colourful picture of a giraffe on the tail. Despite its size it was surrounded by armed guards and we were again making a little piece of history.

The guns looked menacing and several members of our party began to worry whether we would return to Kenya safely. As an optimist I didn't give that any thought, but Dave Brooks and Vinny Crolla were visibly concerned. We climbed the steps onto the aircraft and the guns seemed to be waving us goodbye.

I looked out of the aircraft window and the armed guards were still there. The engines revved and the plane visibly shook. We roared down the runway and up into the sky towards another never-to-be-forgotten adventure.

An hour later we landed in Dar-es-Salaam, the capital of Tanzania, and as we stepped out of the aircraft, we noticed a sea of black faces staring down at us from the airport veranda.

Welcome to Tanzania. I didn't see a smile amongst them. It was midday and the game kicked off later in the afternoon.

A battered coach took us a 45-minute drive to our hotel and it was then that we realised the poverty of Tanzania. It reminded me of Haiti all over again. Haiti was poor and the people lived in fear, yet there was always a trace of the jovial Caribbean in them. Tanzania was different. Poor, yes, but there was a rather forlorn look on their faces.

The country was being supported by China and had a very heavy Communist oppression. The economy was in ruins and there was a general shortage of just about everything.

We were taken to the Kunduci Beach Hotel, one of the best in Dar-es-Salaam. It may have been many years ago, but now it was run down and looking on its last legs. We finally got into our rooms feeling hot and sticky and I looked forward to a nice cool shower.

That was one luxury, however, that the hotel couldn't provide. A shower, yes; water, no. The hotel reception explained that there was a shortage of water and that it would be only on for one hour a day. The only problem was that they didn't know which hour.

We visited the restaurant for lunch. The meal took two hours if you waited for it to be served. It took us only two minutes to decide that it wasn't worth waiting for anyway.

We relaxed before the game feeling hot, sticky and hungry, but managed to keep awake, thanks to the flies. This was a different kind of preparation before the big game!

The top League club in Tanzania, Simba, it means as strong as a lion, were set before us. We travelled to the National Stadium and as we approached the den saw the crowds pouring into the ground. The gates opened and we drove inside. Police with dogs were fighting the crowds back and they weren't afraid to use their batons. It was a frightening scene and everyone on our coach was silenced as we drove around the perimeter of the ground with the crowd inside politely applauding.

I looked round at our inexperienced side. Only Fred Eyre, Dave Brooks, Jimmy Hurst and David Charlton had any experience of the big time in a foreign country. We were about to be fed to the lions.

As was becoming quite normal now before a big game, there was some heavy rain an hour or so before the match and the Simba officials were disappointed at a 14,000 crowd. They expected twice as many people, but it didn't particularly worry me.

The strength and standard of African soccer had recently been emphasised in the World Cup when the Cameroons had done so well in their group. I have said before that the so called little nations of soccer are quickly improving their standards. It had happened so often that we thought we were playing against "also rans" and we were then given a lesson that the nations of the world are coming closer together. All these thoughts crossed my mind as the players got ready for battle.

As the teams took the field I was ushered into the Royal Box having a seat next to the Minister of Foreign Affairs. A large picture of President Julius Nyerere lay behind us. The rain had stopped and the sun made an unwelcome appearance. Large pools of water lay on the running track surrounding the pitch.

We made a good start and after half an hour the scoresheet was blank and we weren't in too much trouble. Our goalkeeper on this trip was Tony Farrow. He is really too small for a goalkeeper, but he said that he made up for his lack of size by his agility. He proved that in this game and became a mini hero.

He was powerless though just before half time when our fullback took too long on the ball and lost possession and we were suddenly one goal down. This goal came at a bad time for us and we fell apart in the second half. We lost 5-1, Fred Eyre putting away a penalty for us.

The best part of the day came after the game when the players had the luxury of a shower with real hot water. The Simba side showed quite a lot of skill but I couldn't help thinking that if we could have taken our full League side we would have obtained a much better result.

We returned to our hotel and our thoughts centred on getting back to Kenya as soon as possible. We were scheduled out of Dar-es-Salaam at 7.00 the following evening. Nobody fancied spending almost another day in Tanzania.

That evening was a quiet one. We were miles from the centre of the town and there was nothing to do but buy expensive drinks from the hotel bar and talk about the game we had just played.

I was sitting in the lounge as a well-built gentleman walked towards me. He introduced himself as the pilot who was to fly our plane back to Mombasa the following day. I brightened up and asked him what the chances were of leaving Dar-es-Salaam first thing in the morning. He went to the telephone to enquire but returned saying that air traffic control wouldn't alter the time.

We were stuck in Tanzania until the following evening, so we would just have to make the best of it. The pilot interested me because he was Swedish. I was wondering why somebody from Sweden should be working for Air Tanzania. Maybe he had been kicked out of Sweden and only Tanzania would employ him. I wasn't sure whether I fancied him piloting our plane. Why should he live in a place like Tanzania when he could have such a higher standard of living in Sweden?

The following morning the sun was shining and it must be said that the beach outside the hotel was brilliant. Pure white sand but deserted with not a person in sight. Our friend, Mr. Thawe, arrived from Simba and said that he wanted to take us on a tour of Dar-es-Salaam.

We clambered aboard the coach and bounced towards the capital city. Parts of it looked as though a bomb had hit it. We were taken to a building that was used as Simba's clubhouse. Outside were hundreds of supporters who must have made this their permanent home as they watched their idols coming and going.

Every country in the world has their football idols. The locals love their footballers and treat them like film stars and Tanzania was no different.

We walked up five flights of stairs to the roof of the building and spent four great hours with our hosts from Simba. We were pleasantly surprised at the friendliness and generosity as for the first time since we had arrived in Tanzania the smile returned to our faces. As much free beer and cokes as we wanted.

The view down below of the day-to-day scene in Dar-es-Salaam brought us all down to earth. I remember seeing a bus rumbling up to a bus stop and it was there ten minutes whilst a massive queue of people fought each other to get on. It was frightening as protocol was completely forgotten. People had only one thought in mind - to get on that bus at any cost. It didn't matter whether you were pushed on the floor and trodden on, as long as you got on that bus. It finally left leaving about 50 people behind and about a dozen clinging on to the sides as if their lives depended upon it.

There was a shortage of buses in Tanzania. As I said before, there was a shortage of apparently everything in Tanzania. However, David Charlton discovered that there was no shortage of mosquitos as he found his body was full of bites when he woke up that morning. A swim in the sea was the only way he could ease his pain and discomfort!

We boarded our plane just before 7.00 that evening and I looked apprehensively into the cockpit where our Swedish friend was checking his take-off. I thought long and hard about the last 48 hours. It had been traumatic to say the least, but I considered it worth every minute. We had gained great experience playing the game and it does nobody any harm to travel and see how the other half live. Comfort in life isn't everything, but the experience of travelling is one of the greatest things in the world.

Our aircraft winged its way into the dark sky and the dull lights below became a blur as we hopefully crawled back to Mombasa. The pilot invited people to visit him in the cockpit and I was one of the first there. I was fascinated with the instrument panels and the work done by the two pilots.

My fear of our Swedish friend had long past and I settled down in the cockpit to help "pilot" our plane back to Kenya. We had lost the match in Tanzania, but we had gained a dramatic victory on the diplomatic front as Parliaments in two countries had helped us to do something nobody else had done for five years. Football has never been the cause of war, but one day it may help to end one.

A visit to Kenya wouldn't be complete without going on safari.

We arranged soon after returning from Dar-es-Salaam to visit the Amboselli Game Park and we made a very early start to an adventure that didn't particularly impress me.

We had a murderous seven-hour journey from our hotel in Mombasa on a coach that bumped its way over 200 miles of rough open track and we were never more thankful than to arrive at our lodge.

After having a late lunch, we boarded our coach again and went on safari. it was difficult finding all the animals, particularly the lions but when we did eventually see one, it wasn't very lively. A buffalo thought differently and tried to make a hole in the side of our coach, before our driver frantically put his foot down on the accelerator and we shot out of distance.

The evening was peaceful but I had a good laugh when I returned to my room to find Fred Eyre already in bed, with a huge mosquito net completely covering him. The mosquitos had no chance of making any impressions on Fred!

The following morning, we were up at 5.30 for another safari and although it was a good experience I was slightly disappointed at not seeing more game. Around mid-morning we made the seven-hour trip back to Mombasa along another 200 miles of bumpy road and again I began to think of the great advantage it would have been to do the journey by air.

Just before we came back we had a glimpse of famous Mount Kilimanjaro. White fluffy clouds hid the snow-capped peak but they gracefully allowed us a peep at one of the world's most exciting mountain ranges.

We try to look cheerful on arrival at Dar Es Salaam Airport despite the stony silence from the watching locals.

19

It's a coup!

W e relaxed in peaceful Mombasa. Friendly people and an air of serenity made me wonder why neighbouring countries had so many internal problems. Little was I to know then that the peace in Kenya was about to get a rude awakening.

Meanwhile we were preparing ourselves for the second game in Mombasa against one of Kenya's top league sides, Kenatco. We lost 3-1 Colin Booth scoring our goal in front of 8,000 people.

This game made me realise how some players think that they are so much better than they really are. The team on this tour wasn't that strong, as I said before, but we had four substitute players raring to get out there and sample the electric atmosphere. Bringing players off is always a hazardous pursuit for any manager, but I wasn't prepared for what followed as I replaced a member of the team with a substitute.

Any professional club would have immediately banned and fined him but we were on holiday and he wasn't even a member of our club. Morale in the whole team reached rock bottom, all due to one player kicking up a fuss about being substituted. He later apologised but the damage had been done.

Later in the week we were scheduled to leave Mombasa for Nairobi and play the champions of Kenya, a team called AFC Leopards. We were then due to leave Nairobi for our flight back to London.

It was Wednesday and we were due to leave for Nairobi on the Thursday with the game on the Friday and a departure back to England on the Sunday. I had had several telephone conversations with Clement Gachanga who was the President of the Kenyan Football Association. I spoke to him on the Tuesday and he was to ring me back on the Wednesday with details of our travel arrangements to Nairobi.

Wednesday was a lazy day as I relaxed by the hotel pool, waiting for that telephone call. The sun was hot, my tan was improving and the only break was having a good laugh watching Vinny Crolla and Dave Brooks both making a terrible attempt to do some wind surfing.

The day slid slowly by and I thought again that we were caught up in the usual inefficiencies of foreign football organisation. I decided to ring Clement Gachanga as time was getting short. There was no reply and as the evening closed in I realised that once again we were involved in the uncertainty of what was going to happen next.

Thursday arrived and first thing in the morning I rang the President's office. His secretary told me that he was out but she would ask him to give me a ring when he came in. Two hours passed by and no telephone calls. I again rang him, but he was still out of the office. For all I knew he may have arranged for us to catch an early morning flight to Nairobi, but on ringing Kenya Airlines they had no record of us being booked on any of their flights that day.

The whole situation was crazy. The press had published that we were playing AFC Leopards on Friday in Nairobi and Clement Gachanga had promised to ring me on the Wednesday with all the travel details. We were completely helpless, being entirely in their hands.

It was difficult for our party to make any arrangements as any minute a telephone call could come saying that we were to get on our way to Nairobi. At this stage the only answer was to decide that we were staying in Mombasa. I still made several telephone calls to Nairobi but the President appeared to have done a moonlight flit.

We settled down to enjoy the rest of our holiday when it suddenly struck me that our airline tickets home were from Nairobi to London and we were still in Mombasa. Our plane home started in Mombasa, called at Nairobi and then continued to London via Rome.

When I contacted Kenya Airlines they said that we would have to board our plane 350 miles away in Nairobi and make our own way there from Mombasa. I have had so many problems over the years with different airlines but most of them try to solve the problem. Kenya Airlines were not as co-operative, despite a two-hour argument in their office on the Friday afternoon.

With the problems of the last few days, I decided that we were getting on that flight in Mombasa whether Kenya Airlines liked it or not.

Saturday came and went and we had an excellent evening with a surprise birthday party for David Charlton. Full marks to the hotel staff who were very helpful in the setting up of a very attractive table.

We were due to leave the hotel at about 1.00 p.m. on Sunday for Mombasa airport and I was up early to improve upon my tan. The scene was peaceful. The palm trees wavered gently in the breeze and the turquoise sea was tranquillity in itself.

I ordered a drink from a waiter and as he served me an ice cool coca cola he even more coolly informed me that there had been a coup. I coolly replied, "What do you mean, a coup?"

"President Moi has been shot in Nairobi and many people have been killed", he replied. "The news is coming in on Tanzanian Radio" he continued.

Eddie Beresford came over to share my horror. "All the airports in Kenya have been closed", he said. Then a smile came across his face as he said, "that means we can stay here a bit longer."

It most certainly did. The Wings representative soon arrived at our hotel to give us the entire full story as he had heard it.

Apparently, all radio and TV has been cut off. There were no telephone calls out of the country, but the aircraft that was to take us home had landed in Mombasa just as the coup was starting in

Nairobi. It had been told to overshoot Nairobi and go straight to Mombasa. It had landed just before the airport had closed. Mombasa airport was surrounded by troops and a curfew was imposed from 5.00 p.m. until morning.

Nairobi was in uproar as all kinds of rumours flew around. We were stranded in our hotel in Mombasa 5,000 miles away from home without radio, TV, telephone or newspapers.

Then it suddenly struck me that we should have been in Nairobi playing football. I later found out that the hotel where we were to stay had been invaded by troops and several guests had been shot. Around our hotel in Mombasa it was so peaceful yet out there, guys were shooting each other! It was difficult to take in what had really happened. Then the peace was shattered. Two fighter planes roared overhead and suddenly a different complexion to the previous serenity appeared on the scene as I took in what was happening.

It was strange that in previous years I had avoided going to Kenya because of the political uncertainty in the countries surrounding it. The one year that I decide it is safe to go, we get caught up in the middle of a coup!

We should have been on our way home but instead we were still lying on the beach. Not a situation to moan about, but the uncertainty of our safety and wondering when we might get home, created an uneasy feeling. The TV set in the hotel reception was playing sombre music with a blank screen staring people in the face. We knew nothing of what was happening in the outside world; in fact, we knew very little what was happening outside our hotel.

The only consolation was that our aircraft was actually in Mombasa so we hoped that as soon as they re-opened the airport, we would be on it.

That evening wasn't a particularly happy one. Keith Bateman and Jimmy Hurst both beat me at pool and the darkness outside seemed to hide the real truth of whether or not the country was being plunged into an internal war.

The following morning, we awoke to find the sun again making everywhere around our hotel looking very beautiful. We were fortunate that our hotel had not thrown us out despite overstaying our welcome. News was still sketchy but it was rumour as opposed to stark facts.

The day dragged on until mid-afternoon when the Wings representative suddenly came hurrying into the hotel.

"We leave in 30 minutes for the airport", he said breathlessly. "Make sure everyone is ready."

I had a quick count of heads to find one missing - Kevin Booth. He had been all night in another hotel with American friends, but his brother, Colin, managed to get a message to him.

We clambered aboard our coach and made the 30-minute drive to the airport. On arrival the place was still surrounded by troops. There was no guarantee that our aircraft would be allowed to leave but word was going around that the airport may be opened for just one hour.

I counted twelve aircraft, all but two were African. After two hours we boarded our Jumbo and appeared to be a lifetime waiting on the tarmac. Darkness fell and then suddenly the aircraft sprung into life, moved forward and very slowly made its way down the runway.

I could imagine the aircraft being followed by trigger-happy troops, but it was a relief to climb high into the sky and wing towards more peaceful countries. The pilot informed us that we could not stop at Nairobi but would be making our way straight to Rome. This meant unfortunately that the plane didn't have any food on board, so we had to travel eight hours on an empty stomach before we arrived in the Italian capital.

Air traffic control in Rome was apparently surprised when we suddenly arrived in their air space as they weren't expecting us. It was the early hours of the morning and after a typically long, excitable argument the Italian authorities brought some ham sandwiches on board for the ravenously hungry passengers.

We arrived in London and the breakfast on the train to Manchester was one of the most enjoyable meals I have ever had. The media were waiting for us in Manchester as we recorded the moments of the last 48 hours.

As the real story later unfolded, the President of Kenya, Daniel Arap Moi, was safe and well as an attempted coup had failed. Rebel air force officers had been involved in an attempt to overthrow the President. Hundreds of people in Nairobi had been killed and there was fierce fighting on the streets.

My unsuccessful attempt to contact Clement Gachanga a few days before the trouble started was a lucky break. If we had travelled to Nairobi, then we would have been stranded there for several more days and risked being shot in our hotel.

We had got through Mombasa airport on our "wrong" tickets, thanks to the chaos there and the lack of airport personnel. Our aircraft had been only one of two allowed out of Kenya before the airport in Mombasa had closed again. We had been very lucky indeed.

Another adventure was over. This trip certainly had its problems, but Kenya and Tanzania had brought new horizons to our touring scene. Diplomatic barriers had been broken and we had been lucky enough to avoid the problems of an internal coup.

Trouble is liable to break out in any part of the world nowadays and there is always a risk that even the most unlikely place is going to be the centre of a political storm. I suppose in some ways it all adds to the excitement!

David Charlton (left) and Colin Booth look apprehensive before the game against Simba in Dar Es Salaam.

20

A new era

Grasmere Rovers had been in existence for 21 years at this stage in 1982 and we always had to hire a ground to play football. For many years we had played on a park pitch, but in later years we had done really well to play on some top-class grounds: Hyde United and Glossop on Saturdays and Edgar Allan on Sundays, later taken over by Clayton Aniline.

It had been an ambition for many years to have our own ground and when I heard that Manchester City were leaving their training ground at Cheadle, I immediately jumped at the chance of applying to Stockport Council for the superb facilities at Park Road.

We finally arrive home. Taken at Piccadilly station after the coup in Kenya had delayed our homecoming in 1982.

With help from Freddie Pye, we managed to get the lease on the ground and so now Park Road Stadium belongs to Grasmere Rovers. It has a 300-seater cantilever stand and the playing area is one of the best in the area. The facilities are excellent and the future has frightening potential.

As a great co-incidence we arranged our opening game on the ground against a foreign team. Jimmy Meadows, the ex-Manchester City fullback and former manager of Stockport County, was in charge of a team called El Saad from Qatar in the Middle East. They were on tour in this country and Jimmy was pleased to bring his team to Cheadle.

We invited the Lord Mayor to be introduced to the teams before the game. He was late in arriving and both teams were lined up on the pitch when his car suddenly pulled up outside the ground. He hurried straight from his car onto the pitch to be introduced to the two teams. We played both countries National Anthems and there was a noticeable surprise on the faces of the El Saad players when they heard their own anthem.

We always try and do things right. It makes for greater enjoyment when events are properly organised. It was good to entertain a team from a foreign country after all the games we had played in different parts of the world.

Freddie Pye took over as President of the club and Jimmy Cumbes was made a Life Member. Freddie was a local lad and we felt it more appropriate that he held the senior post in the club. Jimmy was living down in Birmingham but is still a great friend.

We made a good start to our season in the Manchester League but ended the season rather disastrously although we made another Cup Final appearance. Despite this we decided to make an application to a higher League, the North West Counties League and proposed to change our name to Cheadle Town.

After 22 years as Grasmere Rovers it almost broke my heart to see that name disappear. It was so well known all over the Manchester area and I had seen it grow from a small junior Sunday side. However, progress is part of life and I accepted the fact that we had grown and it was important for our future that we changed our name to one that represented the place in which we played. Cheadle Town was born and Grasmere Rovers was to be just a memory.

We had been on several long-distance trips over the past few years so for the next journey I thought that we would come nearer home and go to Yugoslavia. It gave some people the chance of coming on a trip who couldn't afford the long-distance journeys. It is good to mix these up through the years so that there is always somewhere that will appeal to somebody.

Yugoslavia turned out to be the quietest and most peaceful holiday I have ever had. There were four football games arranged and the organisation of the matches was superb. The coaches were on time, there was no confusion over dates and the teams had everything under control.

This was Jimmy Clark's first overseas trip as manager of the team and despite the organisation soon found that playing football abroad was a different proposition to playing in Manchester. We drew one of the games and lost the other three, but the tour was very low key compared with previous trips.

I just wasn't used to being on one of these overseas tours and not having any problems. I searched behind chairs and in corners, but no problems!

A most enjoyable part of the fortnight was a day trip to my favourite city - Venice. When we arrived there, I decided to go off on my own as I didn't feel particularly well after the boat journey. I had a very enjoyable meal and after being "ripped off" when asked to pay, I tried to make my way back to St. Mark's Square.

Unfortunately, I got lost, but met a Canadian family who were also trying to find St. Mark's Square. We walked and talked together and when we finally reached our "goal" I was surprised when I was asked:

"Why don't you come over to Quebec with your football team next year. You can stay at our house!"

"Thanks for the offer", I replied, "but there will be around 30 of us".

"No problem", replied my new Canadian friend, "we have a big house, so we can accommodate all of you."

I just stood and stared. This was another typical example of how friendly the Canadians were and how big everything was in Canada. He gave me his card and said that they looked forward to seeing us all next year.

There I was in St. Mark's Square, Venice, and I had just received an invitation to take all the team to Canada next year.

On the trip to Yugoslavia was Ian Henderson who was the son of Wally Henderson. Wally had come on that trip to Barcelona and scored in the 17-2 defeat. Ian completed the first father and son to play for the club. Unusually they were entirely different as players. Wally was a big bustling centre forward whilst Ian was a skilful winger.

Glen Buckley was voted Player of the Tour by Roy Venables and Arthur Welsh, but it was a pleasant change to have a nice peaceful holiday. After a busy year in the office and a hectic end of season, it was most welcome.

During the trip we learned that we had been admitted to the North West Counties League. We were on the ladder to much bigger things, but despite this I feel determined that we will walk before we run.

1984 and we were back in the sunny Caribbean. Did I say sunny? We certainly had our fair share of rain as we spent holiday number 23 during St. Lucia's rainy season and were absolutely amazed to find that the locals preferred soccer to cricket.

We have talked so much of how soccer is played and loved in every corner of the world, but I never expected a Caribbean island to prefer football to their more traditional game of cricket.

"There is more excitement", one of the locals told me "We don't mind the one-day cricket matches, but the five-day Test Matches can be so boring".

I was beginning to wonder where I was. Perhaps in St. Lucia they hadn't produced some of the all-time cricketing greats like they had in Jamaica, Barbados and Antigua. Even so we were plunged into the middle of great excitement as Manchester AFC arrived in town.

Their interest in football was even more amazing when a close look at the facts show that St. Lucia were not even members of FIFA. A visit from a representative in February 1984 turned down membership due to lack of facilities and the usual absence of money.

St. Lucia was a beautiful scenic place. The whole island was covered with hills and mountains and any flat areas had quickly been used by the developers for building. They only had one decent ground which is in the capital Castries that they jointly use for football and cricket. The playing surface is excellent except that the centre circle goes straight through the wicket!

The ground is called Mindoo Phillips Stadium, named after a local cricketer who played for the West Indies some 40 years ago. He was an employee of the local Ministry of Sport, who was responsible for our welfare whilst we were in St. Lucia.

In overall charge of the tour was the Minister of Sport, Romanus Lansiquot, and before we left England I was quietly told by the Eastern Caribbean High Commission that the Minister was relying on our tour being a big success so that he would have a better chance of gaining more votes at the next General Election! Nice to be put under that sort of pressure!

The interest in our visit was amazing. We were four hours late arriving in St. Lucia, due to a delay in our connecting flight at Barbados, but at 1.30 in the morning there were still two soccer officials at the airport to greet us. We had four games organised, all at the Mindoo Phillips ground and one thing stood out more than any other. That was the super efficiency and timekeeping that was incredibly spot on. After our other Caribbean experiences that was surprising to say the least.

Our first game was a warm up against a Castries Youth side and we strolled to a 2-0 win. The other three games were against the island's top teams and we did well to win two more games and lose just the one. All the games were broadcast live on radio by a commentator who sounded as though he was reporting on a funeral.

In the one game that we lost, we had a radio on the touchline and it was amusing listening to the commentary. In a one-toned mundane voice, one comment made us all laugh.

"Manchester kick off and the ball is passed back to their captain Larry Gaffney who brings the ball nicely under control, looks round, scratches his head and wonders what to do with the ball next!" Our goal scoring star was Gary Kirkwood who scored a total of six goals including a hat trick in the final game. That more than compensated for his misfortune in Kenya when he fell into a hole on the beach early in the holiday and was ruled out for the rest of the football tour.

Before the game with the National team we had several injuries and struggling to field a full squad.

Gary Conner appeared on local radio and the people of that beautiful island became aware that a team from England was in their midst.

A couple of nights before the game, Gary met two lads in a bar and making conversation Gary asked where they were from.

"We're from England", was the reply.

"Oh great", replied Gary, "whereabouts?"

"We're from Leicestershire". What about you?"

Gary was warming to the conversation.

"From Manchester with a football team."

With a smile, the reply was instant."Oh right. We heard that news on the local radio station."

"Yes, replied Gary, "we have a game in a couple of days and a few of the lads have knocks. Do you play?"

"A little. We'll probably come and watch the game."

"If you fancy getting involved" said Gary, "we have a training session on the beach in the morning so feel free to join in."

"But we're from Leicestershire not Manchester" came the reply.

"It doesn't matter where you're from" said Gary. "Do you play for a team at home?"

"Yes, I do" was the reply.

"Best thing to do" said Gary "is to come down in the morning and we can see whether you are good enough."

"Not sure about that" came a guarded reply.

"What team do you play for in England" asked Gary.

"Leicester City" was the reply.

Gary Conner blushed as he realised he was talking to Gary Lineker!

Larry Gaffney gave one of the best performances I have seen from a captain, on this final game which we won in a nail-biter 5-4. Two players who have played many years for Grasmere made this their first tour, Alan Critchlow and Kevin Malone, but goalkeeper Steve Usher was nominated as "The Player of the Tour".

This visit to St Lucia gave us the chance of putting something back into the game. Coaching schools were arranged for the local school children and several members of our party enjoyed the sessions with hundreds of eager children very willing to learn the basics of our great game.

We were also fortunate to have in our party George Smith and Derek Franklin. George was a member of the Northern Premier League Management Committee and also a Football League Assessor. They took a big interest in the local referees and arranged several talks on the laws of the game and the refereeing system in England. Incredibly in St. Lucia referees are not paid a fee or even expenses. A referee could travel a round trip of 60 miles which would cost him around £5 in petrol but he cannot claim the expenses - a real case of refereeing for love.

One referee we visited at home had a video recording of the Manchester United v Brighton Cup Final and had hundreds of books on football. Being isolated from the hot bed of football can be a problem. George kept in touch with these referees to update them with all the news.

There was a lot of poverty in St. Lucia, more so than in Barbados. Every morning we met on the beach a local 17-year-old lad called Joshua. He became friendly with our party and joined us on the football excursions. The fortnight we were there must have been his holiday too.

He didn't have a job but spent some of his time selling fruit to the tourists. He lived with his grandmother and occupied the kitchen in their small house. The room was very tiny. He didn't have a bed but used a board with a cloth as his blanket. The roof leaked and when it rained he would wake up soaked to the skin. He never saw television or listened to the radio and had never been off the island. His only vision of the outside world was to see the occasional movie. His life savings were 50 EC. Dollars (about £14) which he kept in the bank and proudly said it was earning interest. I asked him what he would do if he was ever fortunate to win a million dollars.

"I would put it in the bank so that it could earn more interest!"

On the final day, eight of our party decided to leave early in the morning for Barbados and a day on the beach before our night flight home. We booked on an early plane from the small local airport in Castries. The airport was deserted and as I searched the sky for our aircraft I soaked up the sun staring at an empty runway. An hour passed by and still no sign of any aircraft. Then someone looking slightly official walked towards me.

"Have you any idea what time our aircraft will be arriving for Barbados", I casually asked.

"I'm just going to get it for you now", was the staggering reply. I stared after him as he dashed away and wondering what he meant and where he was going, I followed him around a corner.

There he was on top of a small ten-seater aircraft with a dipstick in his hand.

"You can get on board now" he cheerfully announced.

We settled down for the 55-minute flight. That was until he found that his radio wasn't working. After sorting out that minor problem, we finally got under way. Barbados seemed to be livelier than it was six years ago. The beaches were much more attractive than St. Lucia, but Barbados comes second best for scenic splendour.

Dave Briody, left, and Chris with the FA Cup. Borrowed of course!

From Burnage to Barcelona - Chris Davies

21

The road to Rio

T
he word 'ambition' features very strongly in this book
and in 1985 it came to the fore once again as I studied a
map of the world. Rio de Janeiro in Brazil kept jumping
out at me. The Maracanã Stadium, Sugar Loaf Mountain and the
Copacabana beach were starting to make an impression.

When I used to look for places we could visit it was always
'countries' that attracted me; now it was 'continents!' South
America hadn't had the pleasure of our company before so maybe
now was the time to visit the soccer-loving nation of Brazil.

The tour turned out to be one of the most amazing adventures
of all.

It was another journey on a Jumbo jet as we winged our way out
of Heathrow to Rio de Janeiro, arriving early morning. Our coach
made its way from the airport to the Hotel Luxor Continental
and on board were some old faithfuls: David Charlton, Eddie
Beresford, Gary Conner, Phil Jackson, Gary Kirkwood and
manager Larry Gaffney.

The Secretary of the Salford Sunday League, Gerry Harris, was
in the party with his wife Betty as well as my good friend Peter
Hollins and his girlfriend Angela Dillon.

We had quite a decent team with us and we really looked
forward to the games that I had managed to arrange. We were to
play the youth teams of top Brazilian sides – Vasco da Gama and
Fluminense. An added bonus was a game against the Brazilian

National Youth team (another National side!) and a trip into unknown territory, Cabo Frio.

The first day was spent resting and recovering from the long journey. The Copacabana beach was just over the road from the hotel and its sweep of four miles stretched into the distance. This of course was where most Brazilian footballers would have started their careers, no doubt barefoot, kicking a ball between the makeshift goalposts littered along the beach.

In the distance Copacabana tailed away into the night where another famous beach, the Ipanema, took its place. This one is less than two miles long, but is situated in a fashionable part of Rio. A song bearing its name was made famous in the 1960s which means bad or dangerous referring to the Atlantic Ocean that ebbs and flows onto its white sand. The lads were soon out with a ball and tiredness was forgotten as they made a stretch of the Copacabana beach their very own.

The following morning at around 7.00 the telephone rang in my room. Not too impressed at being woken up so early whilst on holiday, I just about managed to pick up the receiver.

"Morning Mr Davies, it's Isabel". Oh no, I thought; Isabel was our courier and I certainly didn't fancy talking about excursions so early in the day!

"I'll see you after breakfast" I managed to reply in a grumpy voice, although as it turned out, Isabel Juante was to be a key person on this epic journey. However, more about Isabel later and the incredible contacts and connections she possessed.

Our first game was against Vasco da Gama, before which we were taken on a tour of their magnificent stadium and impressive trophy room. It was a vast area, full of cups, shields and mementoes from around the world. Here was a club with an amazing history and we were proud and honoured to be playing against them.

However, it turned out that we were not to play at their stadium, but on a training pitch adjacent to the ground. Regardless, we were still delighted to be playing our first game in South America against one of their top clubs.

We had a good result against a mixture of youth team players and reserves, losing just 1-0.

The following day Brazil were playing Paraguay in Asuncion in a World Cup qualifying game and my roommate Paul Scanlon and I settled down to watch it on the television. Paul worked for Singleton's, a company next to my office at Fernyhough's, based in King Street, Manchester. We both enjoyed the fantastic quality of football from both sides in an end-to-end thriller of a match. Brazil won the game 2-0, but we were startled when the night sky in Rio was lit up by firecrackers after each goal, caused by passionate locals celebrating their team's goals.

The Brazilian National flavour continued as our next game soon came around. We were to play the youth team of Brazil. Not only were we honoured to play an international team, but to do this in what was probably the most famous footballing country in the world was something else, very special.

The ground where we were to play this game was at the foot of Sugar Loaf Mountain, an extremely picturesque location, which was used by the England team as their training base before the 2014 World Cup in Brazil.

Player Manager, Larry Gaffney, must have been very proud indeed as he led his team onto the field. We lost the match 2-1, with Gary Conner scoring the goal, but unfortunately there was no record of the Brazilian team players; it would have been very interesting indeed to know whether any of these young men went on to play for the senior side.

Chris in Vasco de Gama's vast trophy room, 1985.

22

A very unexpected guest

The return match between Brazil and Paraguay was being played the following day at the Maracanã Stadium and the Brazilian FA kindly gave us 30 tickets for the game.

We were excited to be visiting the Maracanã; it once held 200,000 people in the days before safety certificates, but even now the capacity was around 150,000.

I was in the hotel lounge and Isabel appeared. She had a gentleman with her who she introduced as her husband John. Isabel was Portuguese but John was English.

"Could you get me a ticket for the game tomorrow?" asked John.

"I'm sure that would not be a problem" I replied. "Is it for you?"

"No, my friend Ron" he said.

"OK fine, I replied. "Who's Ron?"

"Ronnie Biggs".

I stared at John and my face must have looked a picture. He smiled and said, "yes, it's who you think it is; he's my best friend."

It took me a few minutes to gain some sort of composure. Then John explained briefly that Ronnie didn't see many English people in Brazil and he would be delighted to meet us all and come to the game.

Ronnie Biggs was an English criminal who in 1963 had been

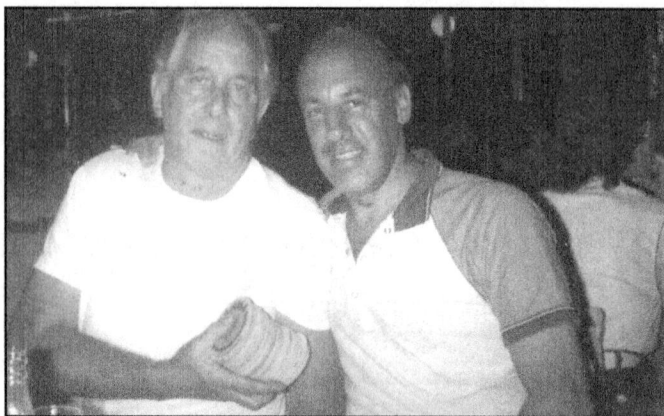

Chris with Ronnie Biggs in a Rio restaurant after the game in 1985.

involved with the Great Train Robbery. He had been in prison for petty thefts where he met a guy called Bruce Reynolds. He was the mastermind behind the Train Robbery and wanted to involve Biggs, offering him £40,000 as his share of the loot. The plan was to halt a Royal Mail train which was transporting bags full of banknotes.

When released from prison they put their plan into action. It worked. They escaped with around £2.4 million which today would be worth over £40 million. During this robbery the driver of the train, Jack Mills, had been attacked with a cosh by one of the gang. He died six years later, aged 65, never really recovering from the shock of his experience. His co-driver, David Whitby, was 25 at the time and whilst he wasn't physically assaulted, he died aged 34 from a heart attack. To this day no-one was ever charged with Jack Mills' beating.

Biggs and a few other gang members were caught, but a large amount of the money was never found. The robbers each received 30 year jail sentences, but Biggs wasn't happy at spending the rest of his life behind bars.

In 1965 several of the robbers escaped from Wandsworth prison by scaling a rope ladder. Biggs reached Paris and had face-changing plastic surgery before moving on to Spain. He then met up with his wife Charmian and two sons before travelling to

Melbourne, Australia. From there they ended up in Brazil. Wow, I don't think that could happen today!

Ronnie Biggs was often front page news and Scotland Yard, who had been given a merry dance with his escapades, sent Sergeant Slipper to Rio to capture this notorious criminal. Sergeant Slipper succeeded, but due to the absence of extradition laws in Brazil, Biggs could not be forced out of the country. However, Slipper managed to get Biggs onto a boat to Barbados from where he hoped to bring him back to Britain.

Enter our new friend, John. Before Slipper could get Biggs onto a plane, John and his friends 'captured' Biggs themselves to take him back to Rio.

Slipper had failed in his mission and Biggs was back in Rio living the high life. Charmian was 'dumped' and he married a Brazilian woman which meant he now had legal rights to remain in Brazil.

The following day everyone was excited at going to the iconic Maracanã Stadium. Our coach arrived and John made an appearance at the hotel with his friend Ronnie, who I thought looked slightly embarrassed as he was introduced to our party.

Our coach departed for the Stadium with our party of 30 people plus one very unexpected guest.

The game kicked off at 5.30pm, but we were told to arrive at the ground early because of the large crowd expected. We arrived at around 3.00pm to an unbelievable atmosphere. To say it was electric was an understatement. It seemed like everyone was carrying a flag, not only that of Brazil, but local team flags representing Vasco da Gama, Flamingo, Fluminese, Botofogo etc. The noise level was amazing as each team group was trying to outshout the rest!

Although we had entered the ground early already it looked almost full. The crowd was later recorded at 147,000.

In today's modern era no-one would ever be part of a football crowd of such magnitude.

I settled down in my seat next to a certain Ronnie Biggs with plenty of time to spend before the kick-off at 5.30pm. To say

I had an absorbing 'chat' with Ronnie was putting it mildly! For obvious reasons I didn't want to mention the Great Train Robbery, but we covered many subjects and I could tell he was thoroughly enjoying the atmosphere within the Stadium.

Ronnie's favourite team was Arsenal, but despite his enjoyable new life in Brazil he said he hoped one day to return to England. In 2001 he did, but on the grounds of ill health and was immediately returned to prison.

Our loveable compassionate rogue died a sick man in 2013, aged 84.

Meanwhile, in the Maracanã stadium, the big kick-off arrived. To be honest, it was a disappointing game and did not merit the big build up. The final score was a 1-1 draw, but it was an unforgettable day, soaking up the atmosphere at one of the world's largest football stadiums.

A few days before the game, I had been in talks with the Brazilian FA that could have resulted in my biggest ever 'coup'.

My mind had gone back to the day when we had had a pre-match in the Aztec stadium in Mexico City, played in front of 65,000 spectators. Our game had preceded the main event of Cruz Azul playing Atlanta.

My plan was to ask the Brazilian FA if we could play a pre-match in the Maracanã before Brazil played Paraguay. I had two meetings with officials and at one stage I was quite hopeful that they would agree to my request. Unfortunately, it wasn't to be, and at the eleventh hour they decided not to proceed, leaving me extremely disappointed not to have received a positive answer.

Had the decision gone the other way, CHEADLE TOWN WOULD HAVE PLAYED BEFORE THE LARGEST CROWD EVER TO WATCH A BRITISH TEAM PLAY FOOTBALL – a record that no-one would ever have beaten. However, with hindsight, I don't really think that our players would have coped with the 'pressure cooker' atmosphere so perhaps the Brazilian FA had done us a favour.

After the game we were taken by our coach to a restaurant recommended by Ronnie where we enjoyed the meal and many hours of reminiscing about the most eventful day that many of us had ever experienced.

Quite surprisingly, Ronnie didn't offer to pay the bill!!

We now move from one fantastic event of watching football in the Maracanã to another – which was Sugar Loaf Mountain and the Statue of Christ the Redeemer. Sugar Loaf Mountain was visible from Copacabana Beach and we were all excited about visiting one of the most iconic sights in the world.

It was my first time in a cable car – and what an experience! We inched slowly towards the summit and the views below were breathtaking. The Mountain which peaks at almost 1,300 feet has panoramic views of Botafogo Beach and Rio de Janeiro stretching for miles.

A scene from the James Bond film, 'Moonraker', was filmed on Sugar Loaf where we saw Roger Moore fighting with 'Jaws' on top of the cable car as it plunged from side to side down the Mountain. It was reassuring to be enclosed inside the car!

If Sugar Loaf Mountain was an incredible experience, then arguably we had an even better one the following day when we visited Corcovado to see the Statue of Christ the Redeemer.

Corcovado is Portuguese for 'Hunchback' and is a short distance from Sugar Loaf. The summit is reached by a 'cog' railway and although it is actually possible to walk along a series of twisting, winding roads, this certainly wasn't recommended!

On reaching the top, the Statue of Christ the Redeemer towers over Rio. It is 100 feet tall and with arms outstretched it seems to be saying to the world "this is all mine!" Never in my life have I seen views as awe inspiring as this one. Johnny Davies lost his cap as the wind took over and was last seen hovering over one of the many beaches that surround Rio … that is the cap, not Johnny! The experience and the views of this iconic Statue were so amazing that we made several more trips to Corcovado during our stay in Rio de Janeiro.

Meanwhile, another match was looming and our third game on this tour was against another famous Brazilian club, Fluminese. This was played in their stadium which although small and compact was very impressive looking, with the crowd close to the pitch.

The four main football clubs in Rio all have their own stadiums, but as they tend to be small, the 'big' matches have to be switched to the Maracanã.

We fared quite well in this game against a mix of reserve and youth team players, going down 1-0. Of course, one thing we have to remember is the heat. Whilst Brazil wasn't as hot as some of the countries we have visited this problem always presents a challenge which can be difficult to overcome.

Our fourth and final game in Brazil turned out to be totally different than the previous three. We were to travel to a place called Cabo Frio which was around 100 miles from Rio, but still in the state of Rio de Janeiro. It is a beautiful place, but we didn't see anything of the town and its beaches before the game as we were taken straight to the ground.

What happened next took us totally by surprise. The coach crawled up to the players' entrance which - when we alighted - was guarded by armed police on either side of the door: Welcome to Cabo Frio! That was the start of taking part in the most frightening match in which I have ever been involved.

The final game on any tour is always difficult: two weeks of sunshine, a few drinks and several late nights do not make an ideal way to prepare!

There were around 2,000 people in the ground and something was telling me that this wasn't going to be just another football match. Hostility was in the air. Each touch of the ball by our players brought jeers from the crowd, although this didn't happen often as a fitter, stronger Cabo Frio team took total control of the game.

I was standing in the technical area, next to the pitch, thinking how I could change the course of the game when I had what was one of the most frightening experiences of my life.

Someone in the crowd behind me threw a firecracker which landed inches from where I stood. It gave an almighty bang and I felt as though the world had come to an end.

How I managed to regain my composure I will never know. I tried to act as though nothing had happened as smoke billowed into the air around me. My stomach felt on fire and I could hear laughter from the crowd behind me. Fred Eyre used to say "laughing at you is worse than booing".

As I had always fancied myself as an actor, I thought that by trying to ignore the situation any potential trouble would be diffused. The police who had guarded us on arrival at the ground were now nowhere to be seen! We went on to lose the game 3-0 but it was a relief to leave the ground alive. However, before we made our way back to Rio the club took us to a restaurant on a beautiful beach area in Cabo Frio.

Our South American journey was coming to an end. Wow, what an experience! … Maracanã, Sugar Loaf, Corcovada, Copacabana, Cabo Frio, firecrackers and certainly not least – Ronnie Biggs. I think I could have done with another holiday after that little lot!

One morning, a couple of weeks later, my phone rang at home and a female voice said:

"Is that you, Chris?"

"Yes, it is," I replied.

"It's Charmian", the voice said. "I've brought a football back for you signed by the Brazilian team".

It was Ronnie Biggs' ex wife; she had returned to England and kindly brought back a fantastic memento of our wonderful tour.

The Raffles Hotel in Singapore.

23

It's all peaceful in Florida

I t isn't unusual that after a hectic tour we follow with something less demanding and slightly more peaceful. We succeeded in doing just that with a two-centre stay in Florida.

We started in Fort Lauderdale and finished in St. Petersburg. One game was arranged in each centre and it was probably one of the few tours where there were no problems.

Rob O'Connor and his girlfriend, Lynne, joined the tour as did Ian Ward. Both were to play significant parts in future tours.

Fort Lauderdale is very close to Disney World and the second visit to this wonderland was equally as good as the first. They add new attractions every year so there is always something different to see. The first game was against Ford Lauderdale where we won 2-1, both goals coming from Rob O'Connor. We then travelled to the other side of Florida to the lovely resort of St. Petersburg where it was so peaceful. Unlike most of our previous tours we felt extremely relaxed.

However, our game here was played against the St. Petersburg Kickers and something told me that the peace was about to be shattered. I was wrong. We lost the game 5-2, but we were certainly not kicked off the park. Rob was on the scoresheet again with also a rare goal from defender, Ian Ward. That concluded game number 78 on tour, but despite it being 'low key' the adrenalin was still pumping for tour number 30 and our 79th game.

Globe-trotting Rovers land Calypso trip

'Rocket' welcome for Grasmere!

24

It's sunshine in Thailand

Two years had passed since 1985 when we had visited the continent of South America and landed in Brazil. As I had said previously – continents were now the new target.

"How about Asia", I thought. We hadn't done it before and in those days, neither had the large professional clubs.

I loved looking at maps of the world and trying to plan our next trip. Asia looked 'ripe' for a tour to remember and after a few months of planning, everything came together to bring about an adventure that arguably was one of the best we had ever experienced.

The idea was to fly to Bangkok in Thailand, play two games, move on to Hong Kong for another game and then travel into the unfamiliar southern part of China hopefully for our final match.

It sounded very complex, but amazingly it turned out to be trouble-free with problems very hard to find. The 'China' part of the tour is revealed later, but that too produced nothing other than an amazing experience.

Our flight from Manchester was to Amsterdam before our connection to Bangkok, with a touchdown in Dubai for refueling It was a short stop so we saw nothing of the United Arab Emirates powerhouse that I have since visited twice which has now become one of my favourite places in the world.

We arrived in Bangkok in the early hours of the morning and

after a fairly straightforward passage through passport, customs and baggage controls we made our way to the waiting coach that would take us to our hotel.

Our luggage was being put on the coach, arranged by a rather fussy guy who turned out to be our courier. Once en route to our hotel, this fussy guy stood at the front of the coach, with a huge smile on his face and said: "Hello everyone, my name is Sunshine". I will always remember that moment. The smile was infectious and he was to become our guide and friend whilst we remained in Thailand.

There was no time for any rest, despite the long journey and feeling extremely tired. The afternoon was spent on a river trip, peacefully sailing past famous landmarks in Bangkok. There was plenty of tropical fruit on board and a drink that was described as 'dynamite'. Heather Garforth had five which, needless to say, she later regretted!

One of the most iconic sights in the world, the King's Palace, was on our agenda to visit the following morning. It was one of the most beautiful buildings I have ever seen and the day will be remembered for the rest of my life.

Our first game in the Far East was against one of the top sides in Thailand called Port Bangkok. We earned an incredible 2-2 draw and even had a last minute goal ruled out for offside. To take in the sights and smells of Bangkok was an incredible experience. Sunshine had introduced us to his pal, Sumo, aptly named due to his bulky build! He accompanied us on most of our travels around the city and his presence helped us to feel extremely safe.

However, it was time to move on and our next location was in the coastal resort of Pattaya. Every room of our beautiful hotel had a sea view and the facilities were top class. Sunshine and Sumo had previously enjoyed our company so much that they had decided to join us on this next leg of the tour.

Efficiency was the key word about all our dealings on this holiday. On arrival at hotels room keys were always ready in reception, everything was on time and we were made to feel so welcome by this extremely friendly Thai nation.

Our next game took place out in the 'sticks' of Pattaya at a place called Bang Saen. Our hosts treated us very well indeed, that is except for the referee!

Colin Booth put us in front and we were hanging on for a famous victory. The referee had played nine minutes over the ninety when Bang Saen equalised. He gave the goal then blew the whistle for full time. I was furious.

On the following day we went to a beautiful coral island where some of the lads went paragliding, but my feet stayed firmly on the sandy beach!

Despite the delightful scenery of Pattaya it was time to move on and the following morning involved an early start for our flight to Hong Kong. We said our sorry goodbyes to Sunshine and Sumo who will always be remembered as great friends.

Our take off from Bangkok was not the most pleasant we had experienced, but was nothing compared to the landing. The old airport was approached by navigating through high rise tower block flats on one side and the South China Sea on the other! Fortunately we survived and staggered off the plane to face another adventure.

Hong Kong in 1987 was under British rule, but what an exciting place. It appeared more humid than Thailand and everything was a lot more expensive.

Our game was against the Hong Kong Police and we lost 1-0. The team and officials were very welcoming and amongst the crowd were two lads from Edgeley, Stockport: Taffy Evans and Dave Edwards After a great reception we were taken back to our hotel in Black Marias!

Again, we didn't have too much time in Hong Kong and tried to cram in as much sightseeing as we could. The best was the cable car ride up to Victoria Peak which gave great views all over Hong Kong. Not quite as good as Corcovado in Rio, but still an amazing experience.

Of course, Hong Kong is now back under Chinese government and I would love to go back one day to sample this amazing metropolis.

From Burnage to Barcelona · Chris Davies

25

Behind the bamboo curtain

There was an air of excitement in the party as we left Hong Kong for China. A three hour train journey took us to the southern city of Guangzhou. As I gazed out of the train window over miles of countryside I was convincing myself with the words: "yes, you really are in China!"

We were only the second club from Great Britain to play football in this vast country, after West Bromwich Albion. Not bad is it – from a small unprofessional team from Manchester? We've had a few 'firsts' over the years, but being second on this occasion was an amazing feat.

We arrived in Guangzhou and following some very rigorous customs/passport control procedures we were met by Tom, our courier. We travelled by coach to our hotel 'The White Swan' – a member of the Leading Hotels in the World - where the Queen had once stayed. As I've said before - only the best for the best!

That evening a banquet had been arranged for us and the team that we were to play in China. Tom had visited me in the afternoon in readiness to translate my speech into Chinese.

I was seated at the banquet's top table, together with Tom, Dave Stevens and a delegation from the Guangzhou Football Club. However, what was to follow proved a very uncomfortable experience! 12 courses of totally unfamiliar Chinese food were served – with only chopsticks as cutlery! Most of it I found unpalatable, but not wishing to be impolite to our hosts, I did

Half a team at the Grand Palace in Bangkok. Left to right: Dave Stevens, Dave Rowley, Eddie Beresford, Ian Ward and Johnny Davies in 1897.

Chris and Dave Stevens as guests of the Chinese FA at a banquet in Guanghzou in 1987.

lots of talking and ate as little as possible, before the plates were whisked away! Chopsticks also proved a problem for most of the lads who looked as if they were having a knitting needle fight with whoever was sitting next to them! However, the last course served was ice cream (with a spoon!) and was certainly worth the wait.

The next morning was taken up with a light training session before resting in the afternoon. We later left the hotel ready for an evening kick-off and I have never seen so many bicycles in and around the city as we travelled to the stadium; there were hundreds.

On arrival, there was an exhibition match taking place at the ground and it made a welcome change for us not to be playing in such an event. This time WE were the main attraction – wow!

As usual, before a big game, I was feeling nervous. Actually losing a match isn't the main problem for me – it's the competing and looking the part that's important – and keeping the scores as close as possible.

The teams walked out onto the pitch to a huge roar and squeals from the 25,000 crowd and the game was being filmed live on television.

As I have said so many times before, it's all about giving players the chance to play football in a foreign country in front of a large crowd. This event was probably the best experience of its kind. Larry Gaffney was our captain and surely this would be a moment he'd remember for the rest of his life.

Although the Chinese Super League had not yet been established at this stage, Guangzhou were one of their elite clubs. The game commenced and we coped really well with the conditions and the quick, short passing movements from our opponents. However, they did score one goal before half time which brought a frenzied roar from the crowd.

Our players did themselves proud in the second half with Rob O'Connor experiencing a near miss with a spectacular overhead kick.

Two goals were conceded in the last five minutes of the game as we wilted in the searing heat and humidity, but the three goal score line could be seen as a moral victory, taking into account the difficult conditions.

The following morning we departed China by train back to Hong Kong, where we had our last opportunity for sightseeing before departing for home the following day. The memories of this fantastic tour will live forever.

74 EXPRESS ADVERTISER, JULY 21, 1988 S

SOCCER IS BACK . . . AND SO ARE CHEADLE TOWN FROM THEIR TRAVELS

Football fan Gandhi!

THE PRIME MINISTER of India, Rarjit Gandhi invited the players and officials of Cheadle Town to his palace in New Delhi after their narrow 1-0 defeat by the champion team of India, Mohum Bagen.

This was only one of the many surprises in store for the team on an eventful tour of the Far East. Gandhi had watched the Cheadle side play on television and as he told chairman Chris Davies: "I like football very much and my son is a football nut."

Amidst heavy security the party of 27 were ushered into the courtyard where four years ago Mrs. Indira Gandhi was shot dead by one of her Gurkha bodyguards.

Earlier Manchester A.F.C., as the Cheadle team is known on foreign soil, played a game which was watched by a crowd of over 15,000 people and shown live on TV to the whole country of 800 million people. The only goal of the game came after seven minutes when goalkeeper Phil Jackson had no chance with a 20 yard volley.

Then came absolutely amazing scenes when a duststorm completely covered the stadium and the game was held up for over half an hour. Advertising hordings were swept high into the air and birds were killed instantly as a wind of hurricane force swept dust and sand from the desert scattering the crowd for cover. It was a frightening scene with complete darkness covering the ground.

When the game resumed Cheadle had several chances of equalising but some good opportunities were thrown away. The local press were most impressed by the performance of David Stevens.

Whilst the Prime Minister of India had said 'yes' to Cheadle Town the Prime Minister of Burma said 'no'. That was the big disappoinment for the team as they left New Delhi for Bangkok to hear that their trip into

mysterious Burma had been called off at the last minute.

Prime Minister Muang Muang Kha decided that, due to the troubles in Burma, it would be too dangerous for the club to go into Rangoon. A crowd of 45,000 people were expected to watch the team play the National XI and the Burmese Government said that the gathering of a large crowd would mean more violence.

A dusk to dawn curfew had been imposed on Rangoon as around 200 people were killed and many more injured in riots against the Communist Government and iron ruler, De Win.

The decision came just in time to prevent Cheadle Town being drawn into a major international incident.

A game was quickly arranged in Thailand against Nakensowan and in temperatures of 90 degrees

26

It's raining sand in Delhi, India

We had fallen in love with the Far East. So much to offer – its beauty, the people, the beaches, the hotel standards, the economy and, of course, the football!

It didn't take long to decide that we would be returning, but with a different itinerary.

Plans were made for a game in Delhi before we travelled on to Bangkok, followed by a ground-breaking visit to Burma, before we relaxed in the beautiful resort of Phuket in Southern Thailand.

It sounded so good, but this was another tour where the unexpected happened and we experienced one of our biggest ever surprises.

June 13th 1988 and here we go again! We travelled from Heathrow to Delhi where we arrived in the early hours of the morning and, despite the time, we were greeted by a delegation from the All Indian Football Federation. We were escorted to the magnificent Taj Mahal Hotel where we were given a typical Indian welcome with garlands wrapped around us and a red circle painted on our foreheads. This is the 'bindi' which symbolises many aspects of the Hindi culture and is said to be the third eye used to ward off bad luck.

One of the first things I have always enjoyed doing when settling down into a hotel bedroom is to turn on the television. It was 3.30am and was somewhat surprised to see that even an old black and white film starring Laurel and Hardy was also popular in India.

However, no rest for the wicked and after very little sleep the lads were up early for a training session under the manager, Larry Gaffney.

It wasn't long before we began to realise how momentous this forthcoming game was going to be. We were to play the champions of India, Mohun Bagan, incredibly a club from Calcutta. Ironically, their journey to the game in Delhi had taken them 14 hours by train; we had travelled from London which had taken us nine!

The match was to mark the Golden Jubilee of the All India Football Federation and coincided with the Centenary of the Mohan Bagan club, plus the 40th anniversary of India's independence.

The souvenir programme contained messages from many people: The Prime Minister, Rajiv Gandhi; Peter Velappan, General Secretary of the Asian Football Confederation; Joao Havelange, FIFA President, plus various Indian Government Ministers.

The game was being held in the Jawaharlal Nehru Stadium in New Delhi which was named after the first Prime Minister of India. It was originally constructed by the Government to host the athletic events and ceremonies of the 1982 Asian Games. The stadium was renovated for the 2010 Commonwealth Games, hosting the opening and closing ceremonies.

We received a police escort to the ground and the stadium looked absolutely magnificent, with different types of bands and dancers providing entertainment prior to kick-off. The game was being televised live throughout India and it would have been fascinating to have known the viewing figures!

I settled down to watch the game from the front row of the stand. There was a crowd of around 15,000, but we made a bad start, conceding a goal after six minutes.

It was then that I noticed some menacing black clouds overhead in a rapidly darkening sky and I decided to move further back under cover. Within minutes, it was raining sand and extremely high winds were causing hurricane-like conditions, forcing metal advertising hoardings to be torn from their fences, lightweight chairs to be lifted off the ground and birds to drop dead out of the sky onto the ground. The players ran from the pitch, spectators sought any cover they could find, as I took in the most terrifying scene I have ever witnessed at a game of football.

However, throughout the whole of this amazing spectacle one of the pre-match bands .... played on!

The calm after the storm came around 30 minutes later, during which time the lads had been sheltering and recovering in the dressing room. Despite the rain, play resumed as if nothing had happened. The score remained at 1-0 as we managed to contain the Indian champions and even create one or two chances for ourselves.

The following morning's newspaper reported that a 'sandstorm' had hit Delhi.

A treasured memory of 1988. Pictured in the grounds of the Indian Prime Minister's home in Delhi. With Rajiv Ghandi are Gary Conner, Clive Rothel, Dave Charlton, Larry Gaffney (resting his chin on the shoulder of the Prime Minister) Mark Fitzgerald, Dave Stevens, Jimmy Hurst, Johnny Davies, Andy King and Ian Ward.

27

Mr Davies, tomorrow you go to...

That evening we were invited to a hotel by the Indian Football Federation for a Presentation of trophies and gifts for our party in an atmosphere that was relaxed, friendly and hospitable. I made a speech to the Indian officials as follows:

….."It is a very great pleasure and a tremendous honour to have this opportunity of congratulating Mohun Bagan in your centenary year. Over a period of 100 years there has been a big change in world football with every nation in the world taking part in this great game.

Success on the field of play can bring great rewards, but the greatest achievement of all is to have that success off the field. Success in making and finding new friendships and - above all - success in helping to bring peace throughout the world by competing at international level.

Manchester AFC have travelled all over the world playing football in 30 different countries. We have made many friends and have brought good tidings to countries big and small.

As you celebrate your golden jubilee remember the people who, 100 years ago, founded your great club. They laid the foundations for the celebrations that now follow.

We bring peace from England to India and the hope that a new friendship can be formed between Manchester and Dehli.

Congratulations on your 100th birthday and as you look forward to your next 100 years we wish you every success.".....

Our captain, Dave Stevens, cut a large cake which had been made to celebrate the occasion.

An Indian official approached the top table and asked Dave for Mr Davies. Dave said that

he had just nipped out of the room:

"I have Mr Gandhi on the 'phone", he said, "and he wants to speak to Mr Davies."

Some of the lads nearby heard the conversation and laughed as they thought this was a 'wind up'."

"Mr Gandhi wants to invite you all to the Palace in the morning", our Indian friend said.

"I don't think that will be possible" replied Dave "as we are all going to the Taj Mahal."

"Mr Gandhi will not be pleased" was the reply.

That was the point at which I walked back into the room to resume my previous conversation with some of the Indian delegation.

I was then aware of someone tapping me on the shoulder. I turned around to see one of the Indian officials who beamed at me and said:

"Mr Davies, tomorrow you go to see the Prime Minister, Mr Rajiv Gandhi".

I stared at him in disbelief trying to find a suitable response. He realised I was in a state of mild shock and repeated the statement.

"All of us", I replied.

"Yes", he said. "Tomorrow morning at 9.00 we will arrange for a coach to transport you to the Palace. Mr Gandhi wants to meet you all." There are few names in the world more famous than Gandhi.

It was incredibly difficult to accept that one of the most famous Heads of State in the world had actually invited the whole team and party members to his home. As Dave said, "diplomatic incident avoided!"

On that memorable day of Thursday 16th June 1988 everyone was up bright and early … that is with the exception of Dave Charlton and Martin Briggs who had overslept and were forced to take a taxi to join the rest of the party.

The coach arrived at our hotel and we boarded for the short journey through Delhi to the Royal Palace. On arrival we had to leave our cameras on the coach. This was obviously disappointing as everyone wanted to take photographs of such a memorable occasion. Luckily, weeks later, the Indian press Association sent me a few copies which will be treasured forever.

We were also body searched before we were allowed into the immaculate grounds. We were then taken to an area where a giant awning allowed us welcome relief from the scorching sun.

We waited some time in expectation before the great man Rajiv Gandhi walked towards us. He shook my hand and said: "I am so pleased to meet you all. I watched the game last night on television and it was a great occasion."

I was so much in awe of such a famous person that I can't really remember what my reply was! He then shook the hand of everyone in the party and insisted that we have a group photograph taken.

Jean Harper recalls that when Mr Gandhi was quite modestly asking where he should stand on this occasion, Martin Briggs replied by saying: "Mr Gandhi, as I'm the best player on this team come and stand next to me!"

Rajiv Gandhi served as the seventh Prime Minister of India from 1984 to 1989. His mother was a former Prime Minister, Indira Gandhi. He was educated at Trinity College, Cambridge, and his grandfather was another famous Indian statesman Pandit Jawaharlal Nehru. In 1966 he became a professional pilot for the state-owned Indian Airlines, but in 1980 reluctantly entered politics at the behest of his mother. On the morning of 31 October 1984 Indira Gandhi was assassinated by two of her bodyguards. Later that day Rajiv Gandhi was appointed India's youngest ever Prime Minister at the age of 40.

On 21 May 1991, while campaigning for the elections, Rajiv Gandhi was cruelly assassinated by a suicide bomber from the

Liberation Tigers of Tamil Eelam (LTTE).

We left the Palace with stars in our eyes as we boarded our coach for another lifetime experience. We were going to the world famous Taj Mahal. Our coach, with extremely uncomfortable wooden seats, took four and a half hours to reach Agra. However, we did have one stop where I remember eating a jam butty!

The Taj Mahal looked absolutely splendid. Again, we were not allowed to take our cameras inside and had to protect the marble flooring with plastic shoe covers.

One of the Seven Wonders of the World, this magnificent edifice was commissioned by Shah Jahan in 1631 to be built in the memory of his wife Mumtaz Mahal, a Persian princess who died giving birth to their 14th child. Construction of the Taj Mahal began in 1632, taking 20,000 men and 22 years to build. This mausoleum is an architectural masterpiece of white marble inlaid with semi-precious stones.

We made our way back to Delhi. What an amazing day it had been: meeting the Indian Prime minister in the morning and visiting the Taj Mahal in the afternoon. Certainly beats sitting at home watching the telly!

Among the many interesting things during that day's lengthy coach journey was the huge difference between our UK roads and those we were travelling on. It wasn't unusual for the driver to be swerving in several directions to avoid various animals strolling or lying in the road; it was like being inside a dodgem car! Fortunately we finally made it back to Delhi airport in one piece, looking forward to the next part of our adventurous journey as we were to become the first English football team to visit Burma.

We were checking in at Delhi airport for our flight to Bangkok when suddenly a voice in very broken English came from a couple of yards away:

"Are you Mr Davies from the Manchester football team?

"Yes I am," I replied.

Three smartly dressed men had approached me.

"We are from the Burmese Embassy here in Delhi" one of them

said. "I'm afraid that we have bad news for you that your trip to Rangoon in Burma will have to be cancelled."

I stared back, open-mouthed.

"Why", I managed to reply.

"There have been student riots in Rangoon and it is considered unsafe for you to travel to Burma.

I was heartbroken. It had taken months to organize that part of the trip. This had included travelling down to London with everyone's passport in order to obtain the necessary visas for entry into the country.

The news quickly travelled around the rest of the party and there was massive disappointment that we were being prevented from travelling to a country where few British people had visited. It was also a huge blow that we were missing yet another milestone of being the first British football team to play there.

Later that evening we arrived in Bangkok and I presented myself early the following morning at the Burmese Embassy, requesting further information. Continuous riots in Rangoon were given as the reason for our cancelled trip, emphasising that a large crowd of football fans would be a perfect target for student rioters and stressing that our safety could not be guaranteed.

During our evening dinner, when we were all together in the hotel, I was shocked to receive a very special visitor: a General from the Burmese Army, resplendent in full uniform. He informed me that he felt it was his duty to travel to Bangkok to fully explain and apologise for the current situation.

The General said that when he arrived at Rangoon airport the flight to Bangkok was full, but he had used his military authority, insisting that one of the passengers be ejected from the flight so he could travel to see us! He explained that a crowd of around 50,000 was expected to attend the game and there would be carnage if the tour wasn't cancelled.

It was impossible to disagree with that!

I read a story in a local newspaper in Bangkok and it is interesting to repeat the graphic account of what it was really like in Burma at that time.

….. "They called it 'The City of Fear'. The advice was not to go out in the midday sun down in the Burmese capital of Rangoon, but with a dusk-to-dawn curfew after recent rioting, it left little time to wander around a country that was going backwards whilst most others were moving forward.

There had been two eruptions that year. Western diplomats in Bangkok said that around 200 people were killed and scores injured in the riots led by students. The latest riot was against the 26 year rule of former General Ne Win and his socialist policies.

One resident said "there are informers everywhere. The same people who criticise the government may report you. You can't trust anyone."

The government imposed a night time curfew for 60 days on the 21st June after the previous months' clashes. Residents had said that patrolling troops had shot dead two or three people caught on the streets after the curfew. "The security guards don't ask questions, they just shoot" said a student who added that he had been afraid to take part in the protests last month.

Men dressed in white shirts and the traditional Burmese sarongs gather on street corners in markets and other public places. Residents tell tourists that they believe the men to be secret police.

Meeting Gandhi.

Criticism of Ne Win's administration is echoed all over Rangoon by young and old, but they all shrug off the possibility of change in government.

"There is nothing we can do. We live from day to day. We have no guns. All we can do is wait until Ne Win dies" said a well-educated 40 year old man. Like all Burmese interviewed in the streets, he refused to give his name.

Little is seen or heard in public of Ne Win, the 77 year old strongman who has ruled the country since 1962. Under his socialist policies most of the economy in resource-rich Burma has gone underground.

Illegal hoarding of goods and black marketing of US dollars have become more frenzied since the government abruptly withdrew 80% of the country's currency – the kyat – in a bid to stifle widespread black-marketing.

"Everyone keeps dollars as a form of savings just in case the government makes their savings of kyats worthless at any time" said one resident. Most traders would offer 40 kyats to the dollar compared with the official rate of six.

Traders complained that their business had been halved since the curfew was imposed. Streets were virtually empty by 4pm as most shops closed for the night and people made their way home.

A few foreign businessmen are still attracted to Burma which abounds in sapphires, jade, teak and agricultural products, but the government coffers are getting little benefit from the wealth. Trade without 'connections' was impossible.

Rangoon, with a population of 3.5 million people, suffers from a basic shortage of most commodities. Black marketeers and youths surround tourists begging them for anything they can spare – pens, lipstick, T-shirts and shoes.

Many residents yearn to leave the country. "Other countries move forward, we go backwards every year" said a resident in his fifties. "In Burma, if you have no money it's no fun. If you have money, it's no fun either," he said".....

Meanwhile I had to extend our stay in Bangkok and our very

helpful Thai friends managed to organise a game for us in the suburbs. Dave Stevens contacted our old friend Sumo, who we met during our trip the previous year, and it was great to have him back with our party.

We now had a few extra days in Bangkok – a wonderful city where there was never a problem in finding something to do.

A 'must' was to visit the Bridge on the River Kwai in Kanchanaburi, on the border between Thailand and Burma. After a two hour bumpy bus journey we arrived at the mouth of the River. During World War II the Japanese military used captured allied Prisoners of War to construct the meter-gauge railway line which runs for 250 miles from Ban Pong in Thailand to Thanbyuzayat, Burma. It became known as 'Death Railway' due to the fact that so many POWs died in horrendous circumstances, many from starvation, continued beatings and dysentery.

This Bridge had become famous all over the world when it was featured in a film based on a book describing its construction. I remembered seeing this film and being thrilled at the steam engine chugging over the bridge. In my childhood my main hobby had been to collect engine numbers which in those days were steam locomotives.

Dave Stevens and I positioned ourselves so we had a good view of a train going over the bridge with cameras at the ready. After what seemed an eternity we heard the sound of a train approaching, but my excitement turned to disappointment as the expected steam train was actually a two coach diesel. The only steam engine I saw was lying idle in a nearby siding!

After the disappointment of not playing in Burma, we managed to arrange a game just outside Bangkok at a place called Nakasawan. Despite the late arrangement of the game, nearly 2,000 people attended. Apparently a loudspeaker van had been touring the area announcing the news that an amateur team from England was in town.

Unfortunately, we lost the game 3-1 in tremendous heat, with Johnny Davies scoring our goal from the penalty spot.

On returning to our hotel we learned that Martin Briggs and Clive

Rothel had left their passports at the ground. Luckily for them, they were found by a Thai official and returned to their owners. Why Martin and Clive had decided to take their passports to the game only they can answer that one!

The next leg of our tour was a two hour journey to Phuket in the southern area of Thailand.

We moved into our base – the beautiful Coral Beach Hotel with great views from its position on the sea coast.

One of the highlights of the week was a trip to the Phi Phi Islands. What an incredible sight and place; just one breathtaking area of many that makes Thailand such an attractive country. The only downside of that day was when our coach broke down en route back to the hotel and taxis had to be arranged.

During our stay in Phuket we played just the one game against a team called Satoon, whose officials wanted to give this fixture quite a 'high profile'. In advance of the occasion we were invited to a local store where journalists and TV media were assembled. Cameras were clicking and scribes were making notes as I made my speech.

Gary Conner gave us the lead in this game, but a last minute penalty given to Satoon made the final result a 1-1 draw. The 'culprit' was Ian Ward who had handled the ball, although he claims he was pushed first and as he fell over the ball hit his hand! Wardy is a great lad and a long-standing friend – I wouldn't want to argue with him!!

A considerable amount of money was made from this fixture, with all proceeds going to a local charity, apparently enough to feed 200 poor children for a year. Such good news was very heart-warming for us all and made every kick of the game worthwhile.

So that was the end of another tour. Great memories, great people – and the football was enjoyable too. Meeting Rajiv Gandhi was as good as it gets and even the disappointment of not playing in Burma could not spoil memories and experiences that will last a lifetime.

As I have said before, I love the Far East and in 2002 I decided to return for a personal holiday. Our base was Penang in Malaysia and one of the ambitions was to take a short flight to Singapore and stay in the iconic Raffles Hotel.

On arrival, the receptionist said:

"When you have settled into your room please come back and see me and I will show you around the hotel."

That was too good an offer to turn down and around half an hour later we returned to the reception area when we were shown around this magnificent building, including one of the top suites.

"John Major stayed in this suite two years ago", he said.

"Is there anyone famous staying in the hotel at the moment?", I replied.

"Mr Davies," he said, "just you".

They certainly know how to impress in Singapore!

PRIME MINISTER

MESSAGE

I am happy to know that the All India Football Federation is organising a Jubilee match between Manchester A.C. of England and Mohan Bagan A.C. of Calcutta on 15th June, 1988 at Jawaharlal Nehru Stadium.

This match is aptly being organised to coincide with an important event in Indian history - the 40th Anniversary of Indian Independence and the Golden Jubilee Celebrations of the All India Football Federation.

Sportsmen have always been ambassadors of peace, friendship and fraternity.

Wishing the match all success.

(Rajiv Gandhi)

New Delhi
June 3, 1988

28

Back to the Aztec

New places, new continents; it was becoming more difficult every year. My mind went back to 1980 when we went on a wonderful trip to Mexico. Sheer bliss in Acapulco and of course our memorable game in the Aztec stadium.

It was now nine years later and I thought it would be a good idea to repeat that tour as we now had a different group of players. I was wanting to give them the experience of playing in the Aztec stadium and a holiday of a lifetime.

Again, the base was Acapulco so I made a telephone call to my friend in Mexico City, Marco Dorantes, the former FIFA referee who had organised our previous Aztec game. He was only too willing to help and he even organised two more very enjoyable games.

Happily, we had retained a friendship with the top Mexican team, Cruz Azul, following our previous game at the Aztec and Marco arranged for us to play the reserve team at their training ground – a wonderful complex with a pitch in pristine condition.

We won the game 4-1 with Gary Conner scoring two goals, Kevin Beswick and an own goal from the opposition, completing a superb performance.

It was then back to Acapulco to continue a great holiday. It is a wonderful resort, but a little like Rio de Janeiro where wandering into the back of the town reveals the poverty that sadly exists.

Our minds were now set on another visit to Mexico City, to play two further games in the Mexican capital. Marco was great and it was extremely helpful to know someone with so much influence. He managed to arrange another game for us in the Aztec stadium, this time against a team of ex Mexican international players. The game was staged to take place before the main event where Cruz Azul were playing a league game against their rivals Monterrey.

Our players were seeing the Aztec for the first time and I will never forget the look on their faces as they walked over the famous turf, looking up into the heavens where the stands seemed to rise forever. Rob O'Connor was our manager on this tour and he did a great job.

This tour comprised a very good team and the lads were brilliant, winning the game 3-1 before a crowd that eventually reached 50,000. Not quite as many as the 65,000 that had seen our first game there nine years previously, but not bad when one considers our players were used to around 100 people back home.

Clive Rothel scored two of the goals and the third was another Gary Conner special. Gary seems to excel in scoring goals on tour!

Managing to arrange a game in such a famous stadium will always be in my memory, but to repeat the experience gives me huge satisfaction. I am sure the lads will remember it forever and, as I've always said, my aim has always been to give players the experience of a lifetime.

We stayed in Mexico City for a further two days as Marco had arranged another game for us. The location was a fantastic stadium, obviously smaller than the Aztec but, as we were to find out, very atmospheric. It was the home of top club Atlanta and, as before, we would be playing in advance of their big league game.

The experience was amazing. The crowd – comprising around 15,000 people - started to arrive well before the game and as their singing and shouting never ceased the noise was incredible. We lost the game 2-1, Rob O'Connor being the scorer, and the players did a lap of honour to great applause from the crowd.

We returned to Acapulco with great memories and so much to

talk about. I will always be indebted to Marco. To know someone of his standing and for him to provide us with so many lasting memories was invaluable.

Sadly, Marco died in 2012, aged 74.

Our final game was played against the local team in Acapulco and we did well to secure a 0-0 draw. Our opponents had enjoyed the match so much they requested a second one and despite our lads feeling extremely weary, following previous games played in intense heat, they agreed. Our opponents won 2-0, but it mattered not. Another great experience had been gained.

One of our players, Paul Connah, who had been so impressed with his experience of life in this part of the world, decided to stay behind in Acapulco. He later moved on to Mexico City and Los Angeles where he became a football coach, before travelling to Australia and settling in Sydney where he still lives.

Despite my many years of organising overseas football tours this task was becoming increasingly more difficult. Everyone had always paid their own way, but the method of how travel companies worked was changing.

The days of booking a tour for around 30 people and being given time to inform the companies of travellers' details - and deposits being paid over a given period - were disappearing. The agents wanted to know details of everyone involved and required full deposits on booking. In these modern times people are reluctant to commit themselves at this stage. The great players who had travelled with us previously were getting older and beginning to move on; the new breed were difficult to pin down!

I had always had help from Halba Travel in Hale who was co-owned by Sir Bobby Charlton and Freddie Pye. They too had moved on and my dreams were becoming difficult to pursue.

29

It's nearer home to Cyprus

The next tour had to be somewhere nearer home and I just about managed to pull a squad together to visit Cyprus. It is an extremely attractive island with very friendly people, but unfortunately it was only possible to arrange one game. It resulted in a 3-2 win with Paul Newton scoring two of the goals.

One highlight of the tour was a cruise to Israel and Egypt. It was my first cruise and I loved every minute.

Ian Ward and I shared a cabin and we tossed a coin for who would sleep in the top bunk. Needless to say I lost! Unfortunately when I climbed up and immediately fell out, I don't think Wardy and I have ever laughed so much in our lives.

The highlight of the trip was a visit to the pyramids. Paul Newton and his girlfriend Rachael - now his wife - plus yours truly made a bad decision to ride on a camel. To say I was terrified was putting it mildly as I was hauled up onto its back, clutching my camera in one hand and being told to hold onto something behind me. Although I felt totally unbalanced, surprisingly I never fell off. Paul said his camel certainly looked worse for wear, but he was obviously enjoying the experience far more than I was!

One thing I will never forget is that as we left Jerusalem in the coach, our guide told us to pull down the blinds on our windows as there was a strong possibility of stones being thrown at our vehicle.

As we headed back to Cairo, our guide gave a very emotional

speech about the troubles in his country. Even then, in 1990, he said: "I don't know if they will ever be resolved."

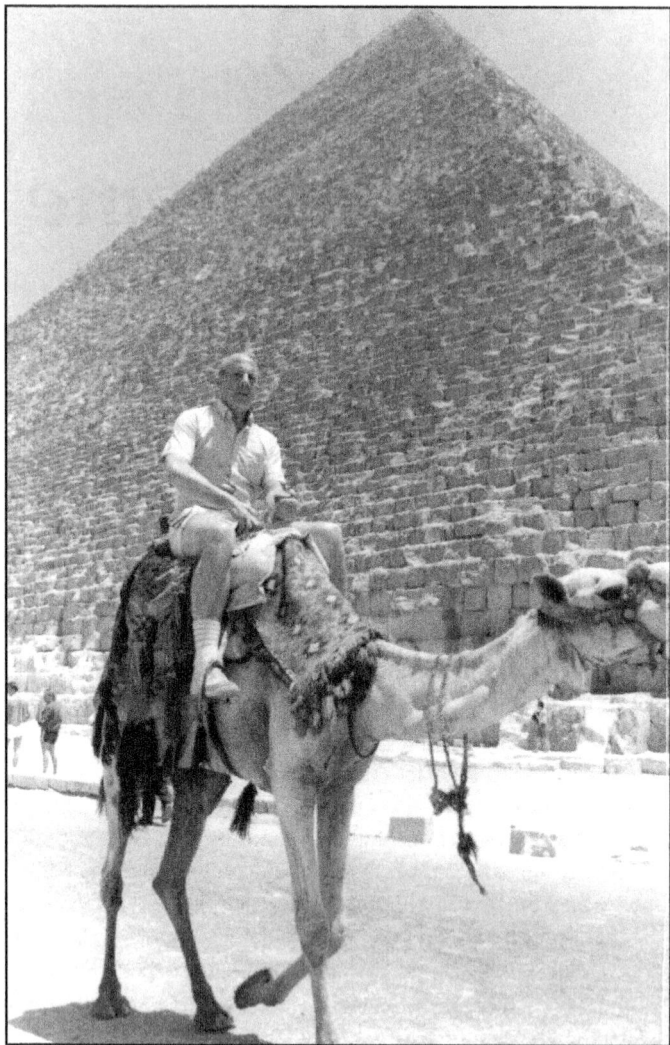

Chris on a camel at The Pyramids.

30

Back to Copacabana

After the problems of low numbers for our Cyprus trip, I thought I would have another attempt to re-kindle enthusiasm for a grand tour!

It was back to Brazil with a new crowd of people to give them the opportunity to visit one of the most amazing countries in the world.

I wrote to the Brazilian Football Federation to tell them we were hoping to return to Rio for another tour. To say I was shocked by the reply is putting it mildly. They said they would be delighted to host us again and would appoint Brazilian football legend Jairzinho to be in charge of our party.

Wow – Jairzinho! He was of course a hero in Brazil, having played with Pele in three World Cup Finals and was the only player to score in every round, including the Final. His given name is Jair Venturo Filho and played in three consecutive World Cup Finals in 1966, 1970 and 1974. He was a right-winger who had a special flair for goal-scoring. The team he mainly played for in Brazil was Botofogo and he had been listed as the 27th greatest ever world player.

Jairzinho played 81 games for Brazil and his son is now making his name as a manager in charge of Pele's former club, Santos. At the time of our visit Jairzinho was in charge of a local club, Sao Cristavao, where he first spotted local hero Ronaldo.

We arrived in Rio, unfortunately not with as strong a side as I would have liked. However, it was a different party from the one who had visited previously and I was hoping to give them the chance of experiencing one of the most exciting cities in the world. The day after our arrival, the great man came to our hotel and I was pleased and relieved that he could speak English.

That was the start of a wonderful fortnight of being in the company of a playing legend. Jairzinho frequently picked me up in his car to show me the wonderful sights of Rio. Our manager on this trip was Ronnie Grabner and he too joined me as we built a playing itinerary into the tour.

Our first game was against our old friends from Vasco da Gama who fielded a good side, beating us 5-1.

For our second game we travelled to play a team called Bangu. They showed no mercy as a strong and extremely quick side annihilated us 6-1.

Finally, we had a game against Jairzinho's side, Sao Cristavao, and again we wilted in the heat going down 5-1. Jairzinho made a call to his great friend, Pele, to see whether or not he could come to meet us, but unfortunately he was out of the country. Never mind – we already had his autograph on the pennant when we played New York Cosmos in 1977 and of course Jairzinho wasn't a bad alternative!

Again, we saw all the magnificent sights of Rio and it is probably my favourite place in the world. The following year I was delighted that Jairzinho accepted my offer to visit England when he hosted a soccer school at Cheadle Town and played in a charity game. He was also the guest at a special dinner I organised, plus another one arranged by Fred Eyre.

During Jairzinho's time in Manchester there was a great opportunity for him to witness a top Premier League game at Old Trafford between Manchester United and Arsenal.

United were tremendous hosts: a pre-match meal, directors' box seats and a meeting with all the players in the dressing rooms before the game. After I had informed Bobby Charlton that Jairzinho was our guest, the two great world famous footballers walked out onto the pitch to a huge ovation from the crowd.

A couple of years later Jairzinho returned to England to work with Wigan Athletic. At that time I had organised another of my dinners for Cheadle Town and our special guest speaker that evening was Frank Worthington.

I hadn't told a soul about my invitation to Jairzinho for him to make an appearance. I grabbed the microphone from our compare Jimmy Wagg, announcing that we had a surprise guest and after five minutes of an introduction, mentioning no names, I announced:

"and a special welcome to ...... Jairzinho."

The room erupted as 150 people saw Jairzinho walk into the room. I enjoyed that!

Over the years I have organised many sportsman dinners for Grasmere/Cheadle Town where we have had many 'greats' over the years as Guest Speakers.

Famous names that would adequately be on any list of footballing legends include: Tommy Docherty, John McGrath, Sir Bobby Charlton, Jack Charlton, Steve Daley, Tommy Smith, Frank McLintock, Norman Whiteside, Fred Eyre, Bobby Kennedy, Steve Kindon, Frank Worthington, Gordon Banks, Wilf McGuinness, Phil Neal, Joe Mercer, Nat Lofthouse, Jimmy Cumbes, Freddie Pye, Jackie Blanchflower, Duncan McKenzie, Denis Law, Paul Fletcher, Gordon Hill, Ron Yeats and John Sillett.

My thanks are due to super agent Alan Platt for his help and the invaluable role he's played over many years.

Chris with Jairzinho.

31

Trials and tribulations

Running a non-league club is time-consuming and often is full of problems around every corner. During my time at Cheadle Town one of the most difficult situations I faced was when the alarm would go off in the clubhouse in the early hours of the morning. It was 'muggins' me who would be woken up by a phone call from the police and I can confirm that it's no fun driving to the site at that time.

The police were not always there when I arrived and the ground was in total darkness, being hidden at the end of a cul-de-sac. It took a brave person to walk into the premises, hoping no-one was around on the attack! These alarm calls became a regular occurrence and the clubhouse suffered much willful damage over many years.

During the summer work never stopped as we faced the challenge of bringing the ground up to standard ready for the annual league inspection.

Over a 20 year period there was a succession of managers, with Paul Cunningham and former Stockport County player, Tony Coyle, being two of the earlier ones. We had ex Bolton Wanderers centre half, Paul Jones, who concentrated on attracting local players and another 'big' name, Gordon Clayton who was a former Manchester United goalkeeper.

Staying with the Manchester United theme, we had ex winger and England international, Gordon Hill, in charge of our youth team.

One evening Gordon hosted a hot pot supper at Cheadle Town where he recalled his many interesting stories to a packed audience hanging on to his every word. However, when the hot pot hadn't arrived at the appointed time I made an anxious telephone call to the chosen catering company – to be informed that it was on its way to Cheadle in Staffordshire, not Stockport!

Peter Blundell, Graham Wright, Steve Brokenbrow and Trevor Howard were all good managers over a number of years. Larry Gaffney gave us great service as a player and manager before Clive Rothel took the reins. My thanks to them all for doing such a terrific job, including former 'Miss Cheadle', Michelle Bowler, who looked after the bar.

The season of 2005/2006 was very special for all the clubs in the North West Counties League. A new club was formed called FC United and they had applied to join. This club was formed by militants opposed to the takeover of Manchester United by the Glazer family. It turned out to be a licence to print money for every club in the League.

Cheadle Town were particularly fortunate in that they were drawn against FC United at home in the first round of the League Cup. The game was made all ticket and played early season. We received applications from all over the country and within a week the game was sold out.

However, ten days before the fixture was due to be played we received a visit from representatives of the Local Council and the League who, despite the sellout, came up with all kinds of reasons why the game shouldn't be held at Park Road, Cheadle. Unfortunately, they held all the aces and there was nothing we could do but to cancel the game.

2,000 tickets had been sold and eventually the game was able to be played at Curzon Ashton the following Monday evening. Over 2,300 people piled into National Park to witness an FC United victory with a score of 5-2.

In November we were due to play FC United again at home in the League and an alternative venue to Park Road had to be found. Luckily, my working at Stockport County helped to secure

Edgeley Park for a Saturday game. In those days Sale Sharks used this venue, but fortunately they – and Stockport County – had away fixtures on the day we were due to play.

What a wonderful day! The crowd was 3,377 and an electric atmosphere produced an exciting 3-3 draw.

It would be remiss of me if I didn't mention the hugely embarrassing 22-0 defeat by the Russian National Under 19 team in 2014.

One of our committee members received a telephone call from an agent asking if we would be interested in playing a 'training game' against the Russians at the superb pitch at Mottram Hall in Cheshire. He accepted the invitation which was to be played the Sunday after our first and reserve teams matches the day before.

Unfortunately, as this request came only days before the proposed game, the manager had very little time to bring a squad together to play the young Russians. Needless to say we failed to field a decent team at such short notice and there were only two players that day with any first team experience.

The result was a very one-sided contest that embarrassed me so much that rather than face the aftermath I left two of our committee members to deal with the TV, press and social media representative - who clearly enjoyed the publicity. I felt as though the club was a laughing stock and I was ashamed to be associated with it.

However, we move on - quickly!

A sportsman's dinner at the club featuring left to right, sponsor John Eardley, Chris Davies, Denis Law, Clive Williams, Jimmy Meadows, Freddie Pye, Larry Gaffney and Alwin Thompson.

32

Stockport County - the good old days

In the late 1980s I left stockbroking to work at my home town football club, Stockport County. One of my main tasks is to look after the referees before and after the game. Going back 20 years or so when we were riding high in the Football League, Edgeley Park saw some of the best referees in the country. Names to remember are: David Elleray, Graham Poll, Neil Barry, Mike Riley and Uriah Rennie, to name but a few. I enjoyed making them feel welcome during their stay and two memories that stand out from most others come to mind.

A week before our game against Middlesborough in the Coca Cola Cup semi-final, an assistant referee told me that the appointed referee for that occasion preferred to drink Earl Grey tea, so from a nearby grocery store I made sure that his favourite beverage was ready and waiting for him! That referee was David Elleray.

However, due to a waterlogged pitch on the day, the match was called off; David Elleray departed soon after the decision had been made and the Earl Grey tea remained in the pot.

A week later the game was re-arranged and I welcomed Mr Elleray back to Edgeley Park. He was taken, along with the other officials, into the room reserved for referees. Refreshments were at the ready, including – of course – a pot of Earl Grey tea, but Mr Elleray hardly seemed to recognise its distinctive taste. "Ah well, you can't win 'em all!" To add insult to injury we lost the match too!

Another story regarding referees happened in the same era. The referee, who shall remain nameless, was in his first season in the Football League and he had a Tuesday night fixture at Edgeley Park. He arrived at around 5.30pm and the first words he said to me were: "where's the nearest chippy?".

Slightly taken aback, I pointed a finger in the direction of a nearby road and off he wandered, returning within minutes, his fish and chips wrapped in an outdated newspaper! This referee went on to have a splendid game and an excellent career at the highest level.

Most of the current Premiership referees have been to Edgeley Park in the days when Stockport County were in the Football League and it's great to see so many progress to the top of the tree.

I remember Michael Oliver when he was in his first season as an Assistant Referee. He was the youngest official in the Football League at the age of 21. I usually have about an hour to an hour and a half with the officials and thoroughly enjoy the pre-match chat about refereeing and football in general. I particularly recall one game when Michael was on the line which was slightly different as he was so shy and hardly spoke a word!

A few years later he had gained promotion to the Football League as a referee and on one particular occasion at Edgeley Park he postponed the match due to an unfit pitch. What a difference! We gathered for coffee - and as many pies as one could eat – with not a pot of Earl Grey tea in sight!

Michael Oliver had changed beyond all recognition and could 'talk for England'. However, I shouldn't say too much on that subject as I was exactly the same, but now I too can also 'talk for England'!

We have even had two referees at Edgeley Park who went on to referee the World Cup Final, namely: Keith Hackett and Howard Webb, not to mention Mark Clattenburg who has also refereed at the highest level, including the Champions' League Final.

Jeff Winter was in charge of one of the best games that County fans had ever seen at Edgeley Park. It was a Tuesday evening when County played Manchester City in a League game – yes a

League game! The ground was crammed to capacity and County won 2-1 in the best atmosphere I have ever experienced at the ground.

No County fan will ever forget the best 'own goal' scored at Edgeley Park which was a bullet header from Ian Dowie of West Ham that powered past his own goalkeeper.

Managers and players who have been at the top level of football have adorned the Edgeley Park players' corridor and I have been fortunate enough to have spoken to them all. Famous familiar names like: Terry Venables, Brian Clough, Harry Rednapp, Tony Adams, Kevin Keegan, Joe Royle, Howard Kendall and Paul Gascoigne. It was particularly amusing to watch Peter Crouch having to duck his head on entering the dressing room, although County legend Kevin Francis also had the same problem. What a tremendous player he was.

These were great times at Edgeley Park and ... one day .... they will be back.

Manager Gordon Clayton (right) receives his Manager of the Month award from sponsors Bass with NWCL official Bob Eccles looking on in 1986.

33

Barrie Dean

It would be remiss of me to write a book about world travels and subsequent stories without mentioning Barrie Dean. If you remember, Barrie was the young lad in the 1960s who knocked on my door and said: "Why can't we start our own football team and you can be the manager?"

I had reluctantly agreed and my life was to take a very different turn from what I had imagined. I know many people have had such an experience as they have chosen one path as opposed to another and their lives have completely changed direction.

When I left school and was searching for a job, I had several interviews in one particular day; the first was in the Royal Exchange Building in Manchester. However, there were about 30 stairs to climb from Cross Street before entering the building - which I found very scary - so I turned my back on that opportunity and accepted the next interview at The Stock Exchange where only one flight of stairs took me to their offices.

I secured the job at The Stock Exchange and I often think how my life could have been so different had I climbed those steps into the Royal Exchange and accepted their offer.

Now back to Barrie. At that time I supported Manchester United and Stockport County and the thought of being involved in amateur football never entered my head. If I had never started Grasmere Rovers I would have missed the wonderful world travels and the pleasure of giving so many young lads the opportunity to play football in huge stadiums in front of thousands of spectators. I have had the pleasure of meeting some very well-known and interesting people that years ago I could only have read about or seen on television:

Alfredo di Stefano and Jairzinho were two of the top players the world has ever seen;

To meet Rajiv Gandhi in New Delhi was mind-boggling;

Whilst some people will make adverse comments about Ronnie Biggs, rightly or wrongly, he was a famous person.

I have taken much pleasure in having given around 400 young lads the opportunity of playing football in a foreign country. I have also enjoyed giving many others, both male and female, the chance to join us on tour. Their support has always meant so much to me – and the players – and many of them are still great friends today.

Also, much closer to home, I have been delighted to have given thousands of footballers the enjoyment of playing competitive matches, whether in the mud of Debdale Park or on the superb pitch we had at Park Road.

There is much memorabilia in the clubhouse at Cheadle Town and I hope that they will stay there for many years to come. It is important that EVERYONE who has been connected with Grasmere Rovers and Cheadle Town is remembered.

Whilst the involvement with football at this level has brought many problems over the years - probably enough to have sunk a battleship! - in life we have to look at the gains AND the losses, but in my case the former certainly outweigh the latter.

Thank you Barrie for everything – and for knocking on my door all those years ago – you changed my life. If good memories are worth their weight in gold then you have helped to make me a very rich man.

Barrie Dean in action on the cinder pitch in Gorton before our first ever game.

From Burnage to Barcelona - Chris Davies

34

Going for the century

W e had played 96 games on foreign soil and I yearned to take that total to 100. However, as I mentioned previously, it was easier said than done.

Then in 2016, during a conversation with Steve Bellis, a Director at Stockport County, the opportunity became a possibility. Steve had links with China through his business dealings and Cheadle Town had already hosted two Chinese teams through his connections. Therefore, Steve was keen to discuss the possibility of taking a team to China during 2017.

The added bonus of this trip was that the Chinese would cover the cost of hotels and travel, with the team paying their own airfares from Manchester to Beijing.

It was a busy 12 months and a flight was booked for a party of 30, including a strong team of players who represented Cheadle Town in the North West Counties League.

Our main contact in China was a business partner of Steve called Peter Gao, but we were being asked for so much detailed information it became difficult to keep up with their requests.

However, with less than a month to go before our departure, we received the tour's itinerary from China, which was incredibly demanding, to say the least. Our last game, which was going to be the big 100th, was arranged to be played the day after the previous one.

Worse was to follow when, with just three weeks to go, we were informed that all members of the party would have to pay around £400 to go towards the hotels and travel costs during our stay.

This was a massive blow as the majority of the players would have difficulty raising that kind of money in such a short space of time. Several had already arranged to take two unpaid weeks off work. We were put in an impossible situation as we tried to raise the £12,000 in 14 days.

With only days to go before our due date to fly, I had to pull the plug and cancel the tour. No blame was being put on Steve Bellis or Peter Gao: only the football authorities in Beijing.

It was a massive disappointment for everyone concerned. I had spent 12 months trying to make this all-important tour happen, but was powerless as circumstances beyond my control overshadowed everything I had tried to achieve. The following week we had a committee meeting at Cheadle Town and naturally this topic was on the agenda.

What happened next I was totally unprepared for as one committee member blasted me personally for the cancellation of the tour. I was extremely shocked and found it difficult to respond as I'm not very good at arguing. I won't mention him by name, but the look in his eyes was quite terrifying. The irony was that he was one of two members on that committee who weren't even going on the trip!

34

Takeover talks

In 2015 Cheadle Town received an approach from a local children's coaching company about a possible merger. It was an interesting proposition and we talked for some time on this happening. They wanted to share our facilities at Park Road stadium plus building a 'dome' on our second pitch which would be used by soccer schools and available for hire by local colleges and individuals.

Most of the money would come from grants and loans and we talked extensively to try to make this venture happen. However, due to an escalation in costs, they withdrew their offer.

A year later we were approached again by the same company, but this time with an offer for a takeover of the club. This was a totally different proposition from the first, but we were still prepared to discuss the various pros and cons.

The coaching company had a contract drawn up by a firm of solicitors, confirming their serious intention of getting involved.

Although the committee at Cheadle Town was generally undecided about the offer, in the main they appeared to be against it. The committee even put forward one or two proposed alterations to the original contract, expecting them to be rejected by the coaching company, but surprisingly they were accepted.

The committee was being put under pressure to make a final decision and everything came to a head at a meeting arranged for 11th December 2017. We had to decide – yes or no. I was still not sure if the takeover was right for the Club and I had several other options in the pipeline. I wanted to delay the process and was fairly confident that this would be the final outcome.

However, several members of the committee who I thought would have voted against the proposal actually changed their minds during the meeting and voted for the takeover.

I was totally stunned and in a pure gut reaction I walked out of the meeting saying I was resigning with immediate effect.

A lifetime's work, love, devotion and dedication were all over in just a few seconds! The curtain had come down on my final act.

Timeline & Statistics

1961	Formed Grasmere Rovers and entered the Manchester and District Sunday Football League in the U16 Division.
1963	First overseas tour to Belgium and Holland.
1964	Played the youth team of CF Barcelona.
1967	Played Elche in Spain who were managed by Alfredo de Stefano.
1970	Played Spartac Varna in Bulgaria in front of 7,000 crowd.
1975	Caribbean tour: played Jamaican national team in Kingston. Only second English team to play in Haiti before 11,000 crowd. First and only English team to play in Cuba. Played national team in front of 25,000 crowd on live TV.
1977	Played New York Cosmos in Giants Stadium. Received pennant signed by Pele.
1980	Played in the Aztec Stadium, Mexico city in front of 65,000 crowd.
1982	Grasmere Rovers changed its name to Cheadle Town and joined the North West Counties League.
1985	Met Ronnie Biggs in Rio de Janeiro. Went to Maracanã Stadium with Ronnie in a crowd of 147,000.
	Almost had agreement with Brazilian FA for a pre-match in the Maracanã Stadium which could have resulted in our playing in front of the biggest crowd ever to watch an English football team.
1987	Became the second English football team to play in China when playing Guanchzou before 25,000 crowd.

1988	Played Mohun Bagan in Delhi before 15,000 crowd and live TV before sandstorm temporarily halted the game. The following day invited to meet Rajiv Gandhi at his palace who had watched the game on live TV.
1989	Played again in the Aztec Stadium in Mexico City before 50,000 people.
1991	Tour of Brazil organised by its former playing legend, Jairzinho.

Games played on tour: 96 in 30 different countries in front of over 312,000 spectators.

Lost more games than won, but the aim was to give local amateur players the opportunity and experience of playing football in a foreign country.

Played under the name of Manchester AFC and always stressed exactly who we were. (Not to be confused with the premier division teams Manchester United or Manchester City!)

Cheadle globe-trotters head for Burma

GLOBE-trotting football club Cheadle Town have pierced the Bamboo Curtain of Burma.

Britain's most-travelled amateurs are boldly going where no team has ever gone before.

Burma has been closed to outsiders for more than 30 years with just a few tourists making it past the border.

By ANDREW CHAPMAN

But tomorrow, Cheadle become the first British side ever to play there and will meet the Burmese national team in Rangoon — even though there's a war going on in the north of the country.

Last Wednesday night they

played in Delhi against Mohun Bagan, one of India's top sides. Then on Thursday, after a quick sneak at the Taj Mahal, they headed for Burma.

Organiser Chris Davies said: "It's a hell of a tour. How many First Division sides could keep up that sort of a pace?"

Since their formation in

1962, Cheadle Town have been on the move and have visited 28 different countries.

Last year they became the first amateur side to play in China, they were the first amateur side to visit Cuba, and in 1981 they played in the Aztec stadium in Mexico City before 65,000 spectators.

Difficulties for the tour when we are denied travelling to Burma.

Kevin Keegan brings his Fulham team to Park Road Stadium for a training session before their league game at Macclesfield Town.

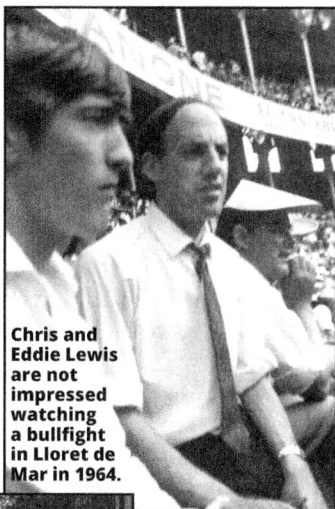

Chris and Eddie Lewis are not impressed watching a bullfight in Lloret de Mar in 1964.

Paul Connah is presented with his NWCFL Player of the Month award by League Chairman Eric Hinchcliffe in 1985.

A reunion in 2001. Left to right: John McArdle, Ralph Lomas, Mike Cuerden, Chris Davies, Keith Towers and Gordon Ramshead.

Small world

One evening in China we were sat in our hotel lounge. Opposite was a guy who began a conversation by asking who were were and what we were doing in China. I explained we were a football club touring the far east.

It turned out he was selling guns to the Chinese. He lived in Australia but told us that he was born in England.

"Whereabouts in England?" I asked.

"A place called Stockport, just outside Manchester" he replied.

Intrigued at the coincidence of meeting someone in China who used to live in Stockport, I asked him whereabouts in Stockport. His answer knocked me back.

"A place called Cheadle".

"You're joking?" I exclaimed.

"No, I used to live on Brookfield Road".

"That's amazing, Brookfield Road is right next to the football ground where we play" I replied.

"Is that the ground with the small stand on the halfway line?" he enquired.

"Yes" I replined, even more amazed. Then he came back with something that left me incredulous:

"My father helped to build that stand back in 1934."

There we were, 6,000 miles away in China speaking to a guy whose father had helped to build the stand n our ground. It doesn't get any more amazing that that!

Tributes to Chris Davies

"You opened up many opportunities for lots of people. You have been amazing. I feel so proud to know you. You are one of the nicest men I know." Angie Withers

"Well done for all the great work you have done over the last 50 years." Brian Simpson

"Be proud in what you have done; there aren't many people like you." Roy Reed

"You should be extremely proud of your achievements. Your forward vision and hard work have had a positive influence on many of our lives." Doug Welsh

"In 1968 when I joined Grasmere Rovers for my first tour, little did I know what a huge influence this would have on my life, continuing to this day. Your dedication, enthusiasm and hard work has been amazing. Thank you for your special friendship - long may it continue." Jean Harper

"Nobody could have done so much for so long with your commitment. You have given so many players so much enjoyment and we owe you a debt of gratitude." Ian Ward

"You've done a fantastic job for amateur footballers and you have the love and respect of many people who are now better after being guided by your enthusiasm." Ian Holland

"There are many footballers who will be ever grateful for the opportunities you provided them and particularly the happy memories of playing abroad." Ronnie Grabner

Printed in Dunstable, United Kingdom

64823970R00151